The

RULES *of*
ENGAGEMENT

for

OVERCOMING
YOUR PAST

CINDY TRIMM
BEST-SELLING AUTHOR OF *COMMANDING YOUR MORNING*

CHARISMA
HOUSE

THE RULES OF ENGAGEMENT FOR OVERCOMING YOUR PAST
  by Cindy Trimm
Published by Charisma House
Charisma Media/Charisma House Book Group
600 Rinehart Road
Lake Mary, Florida 32746
www.charismahouse.com

Cover design by Justin Evans
Design Director: Bill Johnson

Visit the author's website at www.cindytrimm.com.

Library of Congress Cataloging-in-Publication Data:
An application to register this book for cataloging has been submitted to the Library of Congress.
International Standard Book Number: 978-1-62136-233-3
E-book ISBN: 978-1-62136-234-0

This publication is translated in Spanish under the title *Las reglas de combate para derrotar tu pasado*, copyright © 2014 by Cindy Trimm, published by Casa Creación, a Charisma Media company. All rights reserved.

14 15 16 17 18 — 9 8 7 6 5 4 3 2
Printed in the United States of America

CONTENTS

INTRODUCTION

*Remember ye not the former things, neither consider
the things of old. Behold, I will do a new thing; now it
shall spring forth; shall ye not know it? I will even make
a way in the wilderness, and rivers in the desert.*
—ISAIAH 43:18–19, KJV

I BELIEVE WE ARE in a time of great transition that
is bringing incredible shifts and changes. As I was
praying near the beginning of the year, I sensed that
the Lord would be ushering in and bringing forth the
new. But if we are to fully embrace the new, it is imper-
ative that we first walk out of the old. Indeed, we must
overcome the past if we are ever to move forward.

This is not a simple process. If it was easy to gain vic-
tory over past mistakes, abuse, betrayal, trauma, or the
like, everyone would do it. But overcoming the past
requires intentional effort. It requires key strategies
and techniques that must be implemented through
prayer, and it requires diligence to persevere through
the emotional discomfort change brings. That is why I
have written *The Rules of Engagement for Overcoming
Your Past*—to give you tools that will help you break

free from the old ways of thinking, believing, and acting that are keeping you chained to the past. The "past" is an interesting concept. It is used to indicate the totality of events that occurred before a given point in time. The term is derived from the linear way in which human beings experience time, and

> If we are to fully embrace the new, it is imperative that we walk out of the old.

it is accessed through memory and recollection. There are aspects of the past that we remember with great joy, and these memories give us strength and momentum to prosper and move forward in life. But there are also aspects of the past that serve to weigh us down and prevent us from progressing, thus strongly contending with our success in both the present and future.

It is the latter aspect of the past that requires skillful dealing in order for you to be propelled into a bright, prosperous, productive, holistically successful future. This will occur through prayer and the leading of the Holy Spirit, who will give you directives tailored to address the specific challenges and situations you face.

When discussing leaving the old and embracing the new, Isaiah 43:19 is often quoted: "Behold, I will do a new thing; now it shall spring forth; shall ye not know it? I will even make a way in the wilderness, and rivers in the desert" (KJV). I believe it is important to note that before this divine pronouncement of the "new" is a directive to "remember ye not the former things, neither consider the things of old" (v. 18, KJV).

Given that the past is accessed through memory and recollection, it is interesting that this verse tells us to "remember not" the former things in order to rid ourselves of them. In other words, if we choose to obey this divine instruction and stop ruminating on the past, it can be detached from us and, as a result, lose its ability to impact us in the present or future.

To forget the old and move confidently into the new we must address strongholds—those influences that diametrically oppose the kingdom of God—and the demonic spirits that seek to keep us bound and ineffective. In *The Rules of Engagement for Overcoming Your Past* you will find a robust and practical approach to address and overcome these adverse spiritual influences. It will show you how to embrace change and alter the patterns that have yielded the same unwanted results again and again.

Michael Miles, author of *Thirty Days to Change Your Life*, once wrote, "The present is always fresh. There is always a new choice to make, and you are always creating your life again. No matter what has happened in the past—whatever habits you have developed, however deeply ingrained are your patterns of behavior—there is always scope for you to choose a new response."[1]

Each of us is given the opportunity to change, and it should not be missed or taken for granted. God wants to do a new thing in your life, and that begins with releasing the past. Choosing to overcome the past is a destiny-altering decision. For those who are willing to release the pain of guilt or shame, abuse or abandonment, betrayal or rejection, transformation awaits.

CHAPTER 1

ARE YOU READY FOR THE CHALLENGE?

*If the Son therefore shall make you
free, ye shall be free indeed.*
—JOHN 8:36, KJV

WHEN JONI EARECKSON TADA was seventeen years old, a diving accident left her paralyzed from the shoulders down. Lying in a hospital bed in the summer of 1967, she was "desperately trying to make ends meet, desperately trying to turn [her] right side down emotions, right side up."[1]

She writes:

> In my pain and despair, I had begged many of my friends to assist me in suicide. That seems to be a common topic these days and many disabled people that I know even in the nineties have a tough time finding life worth living. I sought to find a final escape, a final solution, through assisted suicide, begging my friends to slit my wrists, dump pills down my throat, anything to end my misery. The source of my depression is understandable. I could not face the prospect of

> sitting down for the rest of my life without use of
> my hands, without use of my legs. All my hopes
> seem dashed. My faith was shipwrecked....I was
> numb emotionally, desperately alone, and so very,
> very frightened.[2]

Angry and unsure of her future, Joni was full of questions: Why did God allow this to happen? How could this be part of His plan for her life?

> Most of the questions I asked, in the early days
> of my paralysis, were questions voiced out of a
> clenched fist, an emotional release, an outburst
> of anger. I don't know how sincere my questions
> really were. I was just angry. But after many
> months those clench fists questions became ques-
> tions of a searching heart. I sincerely and hon-
> estly wanted to find answers....I needed a friend
> who would help me sort through my emotions,
> who would help bring me out of the social isola-
> tion, who would help me deal with the anger. A
> friend who would point me somewhere, anywhere,
> in God's Word to help me find answers.[3]

We may not all be able to relate to the turmoil caused by the news of complete paralysis, but most of us know how it feels to struggle for answers to life's painful events. Who among us has not felt the pain of losing something or someone? Who among us has not grieved that loss and wished life could go back to the way it was—when we felt "normal" and in control of what was happening in and around us? Like Joni, we wrestle with frustration, anger, and despair. We want to serve God, but we find ourselves spiritually paralyzed and emotionally handicapped, unable to break free from the things that bind us to our pain and imprison our joy and peace.

In Romans chapter 7 we find the apostle Paul bemoaning his struggle for freedom from psychological and spiritual torment. He longs to do what is right but finds his life misaligned with the will of God again and again. He describes his frustrated state as a third party observer would. He is in agony as sin relentlessly summons and seduces his fallen nature and he responds like a puppet to the tugs of an invisible puppeteer. At last he makes a profound declaration followed by a soul-searching question, categorically stating:

> I have discovered this principle of life—that when I want to do what is right, I inevitably do what is wrong. I love God's law with all my heart. But there is another power within me that is at war with my mind. This power makes me a slave to the sin that is still within me. Oh, what a miserable person I am! Who will free me from this life that is dominated by sin and death? Thank God! The answer is in Jesus Christ our Lord.
>
> —ROMANS 7:21–25, NLT

We each are confronted with our own similar dilemmas as we pray for divine strategies to help us live victoriously. Like Paul, we want to be free from the things that keep us bound or stuck in the past. We want freedom from the pain and paralysis sustained from accidents or illnesses. We want freedom from emotional hurts, betrayal, rejection, addictions, bitterness, anxiety, and all kinds of fears. We want freedom from bondage to emotionally and psychologically debilitating habits and from all types of abuse—physical, emotional, and verbal. We want freedom from guilt, rage, and anger. We want freedom from debt, shame, embarrassment, and most of all from the accompanying condemnation.

You don't have to merely long for this liberty. Like Joni and Paul the Apostle, you too can find your freedom in God through Jesus Christ our Lord (1 Cor. 15:57). He came to liberate you from all forms of bondage. He has come to release you to become all that God designed you to be.

TRUE FREEDOM

Some people think freedom is the right to do whatever they want. They have the right to say whatever they think, do whatever they feel like doing, put into their bodies whatever they desire, allow into their minds whatever they find entertaining, and go wherever they think they will have a good time. This comes with just one caveat—that their actions shouldn't hurt any other non-consenting, of-age, mentally competent individual.

Freedom means something different to me. It is the ability to say no when yes is easier and more convenient. If you do not have the power to say no and to follow through with the corresponding action, you are not free but bound. Being able to say no to wrong and inappropriate things means you can say yes to right and appropriate things. This is freedom. People who are bound are stuck doing the wrong things when they want to do right.

Many people think there are too many laws and that these laws infringe upon their freedom. They think laws should be instituted to protect people from predators, criminals, or exploiters, but beyond that individuals should be able to basically do or say whatever makes them happy. In fact, more and more people are arguing to change laws governing prostitution, drug use, censorship, and other activities traditionally considered harmful. They say, "If people want to do that, isn't it their own business as long as it doesn't hurt anyone else?"

I find that this kind of "freedom" is really bondage. Beneath the arguments in favor of legalizing prostitution or marijuana use, the real question being asked is this: If you and I are simply physical bodies interacting with a physical world and have only one shot at existence, shouldn't we get as much pleasure out of life as we can? The problem with this thinking is that we are more than just physical bodies. We have a soul and a spirit governed by spiritual laws and not natural ones. (See Joshua 1:8–9; Romans 8:2.) What if there is more to freedom than doing whatever you want? If indulging in certain activities leaves you feeling hollow and disgusted with yourself instead of bringing the satisfaction they promised, is that really freedom?

You are more than what you see on the outside. Who you really are—your true value—is found on the inside. (See 2 Corinthians 4:7.) True freedom is found not in pursuing what is pleasurable to your body and its five physical senses but in what is healthy and edifying to your soul. "Laws and principles," wrote Charlotte Brontë, "are not for the times when there is no temptation: they are for such moments as this, when body and soul rise in mutiny against their rigour....If at my individual convenience I might break them, what would be their worth?"[4]

A WAY OUT

If you cannot say no to an emotion, relationship, behavior, or the like, you are not free but bound. The apostle Paul describes what it is like to be stuck in a pattern you cannot escape:

> For what I am doing, I do not understand; for I am not practicing what I would like to do, but I am doing the very thing I hate....For I know that nothing good dwells in me...for the willing [to live right] is present in me, but the doing of the good is not. For the good that I want, I do not do, but I practice the very evil that I do not want.
> —ROMANS 7:15, 18–19, NAS

Anyone who has been trapped in a cycle of unwanted behavior can identify with this passage. Even in the midst of the act we sense ourselves losing the struggle to overcome our self-defeating habits, incapacitating emotional pain, and debilitating addictions to the persistence of our cravings. Weak-willed, we seek the momentary satisfaction of taking that drug; drinking that shot to mitigate the pain, depression, and despondency; or eating that extra helping (or third or fourth!) to comfort our souls. We cut down that coworker to show her who really has the power. We talk behind the back of that friend who has betrayed us. We belittle those in authority who have abused us organizationally, corporately, or personally. We click back to that pornographic website for self-pleasure because seeking connection with others is too painful.

We abuse those we say we love because we have neither the integrity nor the emotional reserves to accept personal responsibility and deal with our shame and self-hatred. We give in to the urge to reach one more level in that video game. We light just one more "last" cigarette, linger those extra minutes away from our workstations, stay that much later at the office rather than face the pressures at home, savor that grudge, justify not forgiving or trusting someone, or any of a number of other things that keep us from addressing the things that are preventing us from living a life of joy, fulfillment, and purpose.

As we make decisions we know are not the most appropriate, we undermine our own greatness, believing the lies that "nothing good dwells in me" and that we are neither good enough nor strong enough to do any better. We dismiss our errant proclivities by saying, "I'm only human," as if being human means we cannot overcome our weaknesses. You are created in the image and likeness of God. He did not create you to go through life flawed but fabulous.

But without the proper tools, no matter how hard we will ourselves to do right, we still don't seem to succeed. The good we want to do, we don't do, and the evil we don't want to do, we do. We fight a battle—a seemingly losing battle—within ourselves. We think we must be beyond help. The bad within us is too strong, and we are doomed to live in this downward cycle for the rest of our lives. And so we throw in the proverbial towel.

> **You can make a decision today to rid yourself of the pain of yesterday so that you can live with peace tomorrow.**

We tell ourselves, "If it is not one thing it's another." We get over one hurdle only to see another one just around the corner and we think, "This is as good as it gets." "Things will never change." "It doesn't make sense trying to get up; I always get knocked down." "I never get a break."

If you have ever felt even a tinge of this, I am here to tell you that you are being deceived. The person Paul describes in Romans 7 is not someone beyond hope, it is simply a person who has yet to embrace the power to change that Jesus Christ wants to give each of us. That person in Romans 7 is not a hopeless individual—but the person we all are without the liberating power of Christ in our lives.

I am not saying that addictions, habits, dysfunction, abuse, and codependency aren't real. I am saying, more importantly, that liberty from these conditions is available. The price has been paid that we might be free to be the change we want to see in the world. But if we remain ignorant of how to accept what God has already provided for us, we will never step into the richness of all we were created to be.

Those of us who live in America often take our national and individual freedom for granted. There are so many who would risk their lives to have the freedom we enjoy. They live in daily fear because their rights have been robbed from them by oppressive governments, or worse still, anti-government rebels.

So I ask, what is your true freedom worth to you? You can make a decision today to rid yourself of the pain of yesterday so that you can live with peace tomorrow.

To do so, you must learn a new way of dealing with old pain and problems. You will have to trust the Lord as He guides you through a path that at times will seem counterintuitive. Yet in the end you will look back on the journey with gratitude that you, like every freedom fighter, were willing to fight your way from a place of bondage to a new place in God—a place of freedom. Here within these pages are your rules of engagement.

Are you up for that challenge? Are you ready to be truly free? If so, the first thing you need to understand is why you are stuck in your current dilemma. Then you can begin to explore how to take hold of everything Jesus provided to get you out.

If you feel despondent, discouraged, or hopeless at this very moment, bow your head and commit your life and situation to God. Pray this simple prayer:

Lord Jesus, I commit my life and this situation to You. Forgive me for trying to do this alone. I accept Jesus as my Lord and Savior. Heal me of my pain. Deliver me from the hands of my enemies. Grant me the peace in my heart that I need today. Give me wisdom to make the right decision and the resilience to resist the temptation to cave in under the pressure. Give me the strength to say no to the wrong things so that I may say yes to the right things. Amen.

For the moment all discipline seems
painful rather than pleasant, but later it
yields the peaceful fruit of righteousness
to those who have been trained by it.

—HEBREWS 12:11, ESV

CHAPTER 2

REWIRING YOUR MIND

The significant problems we face cannot be solved at the same level of thinking we were at when we created them.[1]
—**ALBERT EINSTEIN**

HELEN KELLER WAS just eighteen months old when she lost both her hearing and her sight. Frustrated by her inability to communicate, Helen became a wild and unruly child, tormenting her parents and relatives. Those around her had no idea what she would become. She would scratch, bite, hit, and punch other people when she was angry. Some relatives called her a monster, and her parents were encouraged to put her in an institution.

That was before she met Anne Sullivan. The teacher showed her that she could do the things others said she couldn't—she would learn to talk, read lips with her fingers, and even write. Describing the first time she understood a word—water—Keller said, "Suddenly I felt a misty consciousness as of something forgotten—a thrill of returning thought; and somehow the mystery of language was revealed to me. I knew then that 'w-a-t-e-r' meant the wonderful cool something that was flowing over my hand. That living word awakened my soul, gave it light, hope, joy, set it free!"[2]

The change in Keller's mind changed the course of her life. Keller became determined to push past her physical limitations, attending school and becoming the first blind-deaf person to graduate from Radcliffe College. She later wrote a dozen books and became a noted speaker, traveling widely as an advocate for people with disabilities. "The only thing worse than being blind," Keller once said, "is having sight but no vision."[3] Through her sheer will and grit, Keller gained freedom from her disability by training a body once defined by its limitations to serve her rather than hold her captive.

Like Keller, if you want to see new changes in your life, you must alter the paradigms that shape your belief system. That begins with changing how you see yourself. You must see yourself from God's perspective—as a human being capable of change. When you change your concept of yourself and the context from which you view yourself, you will discover the power to transform your life.

Carl Jung once said, "Your vision will become clear only when you can look into your own heart. Who looks outside, dreams; who looks inside, awakes."[4] It would be a shame for you to go through life blind to the fact that you are not powerless. You have God's divine power within, and that is stronger than any debilitating power without. You are powerful beyond your ability to comprehend. God is working within you both to will and to do of His good pleasure (Phil. 2:13). You are not a slave to your body nor powerless over your desires; your body is a slave to you.

In the first earthly encounter Jesus had with Satan, their struggle was over power and who would control the kingdoms on the earth for all eternity (Matt. 4:1–11). This is the same battle the devil is fighting with us today. Remember, Satan is the prince of the power of the air and not the earth. He is an imposter as well as an impersonator. He does not have legal right to operate in the earth realm, but you do. Psalm 115:15–16 states that we "are blessed of the LORD which made heaven and earth. The heaven, even the heavens, are the LORD's: but the earth hath he given to the children of men" (KJV).

If you were to see yourself from God's perspective, you would realize that you have been given divine power and spiritual authority to accomplish God's purposes in the earth (Luke 10:19). In order to walk in the fullness of who God created you to be, you must reclaim the authority you've been given and see yourself the way God sees you. This will require the rewiring of your mind. The apostle Paul refers to this in Ephesians 4:23 as being "renewed in the spirit of your mind."

When the enemy tempted Jesus in Matthew 4, he attacked His mind—namely, His perception and imagination. But Jesus did not entertain the devil's claims as truth. Jesus knew Satan wanted Him to question who He was, and He never bought into the devil's lies or let him play mind games. Jesus knew that He already possessed what the enemy was offering Him.

In the same way, Satan's aim is to steal what already belongs to you. The enemy spends his time negotiating with you in an attempt to get you to give up something more valuable than what he is offering—your personal power and spiritual authority. Revelation 11:15 tells us that "the kingdoms of this world are become the kingdoms of our Lord, and of his Christ; and he shall reign for ever and ever" (KJV). As a member of God's family, you are a kingdom citizen. God has delivered you from the kingdom of darkness and brought you into the kingdom of light (Col. 1:13). Don't allow the enemy to play games with your mind. You are not a product of your environment. You are an overcomer in Christ.

Satan is the original identity thief. If you give him your mind and emotions, he will control your life. Like a master puppeteer he will take charge of your:

- Marriage
- Relationships
- Destiny
- Finances
- Quality of life
- Business
- Career path
- Fatherhood

- Motherhood
- And anything else he can access.

As a kingdom citizen no weapon formed against you will prosper (Isa. 54:17) because your spiritual weapons are far superior to the enemy's weapons. According to 2 Corinthians 10:4–5, they are "mighty in God for pulling down strongholds." You have been equipped to cast down "arguments and every high thing that exalts itself against the knowledge of God" by "bringing every thought into captivity to the obedience of Christ." Even as Jesus resisted the enemy you must remember that you have the mind of Christ, which means you have the power to resist the enemy with a renewed mind-set (Phil. 2:5; 1 Cor. 2:16). You are no longer fighting this battle from the old place of defeat but from a new place: the kingdom of heaven, which is far superior to the kingdom of darkness you were delivered from (Col. 1:12–13).

SHIFTING YOUR PARADIGMS

In order to maximize the spiritual weapons made available to you, Jesus explicitly states that you must live a repented life (Matt. 4:17; Acts 3:19). Repentance is often confused with confession. Confession is taking responsibility for unrighteous thoughts, words, or actions. Repentance is something more. It suggests a paradigm shift: a change in mind-set, a restoration of thought processes, and a returning to the way God originally created you to think. This new way of thinking leads to a change in behavior.

Simply put, confession is acknowledging sin, which positions you to receive forgiveness. Repentance rewires the mind so that you never commit the sin again.

Oliver Wendell Holmes once said, "Every now and then a man's mind is stretched by a new idea or sensation, and never shrinks back to its former dimensions."[5] This is what should happen when we receive the message of the kingdom. God made you a thinking being, and He has given you the power to think for a change.

Before your born-again experience, you had paradigms that contributed to your decision-making processes. Those decisions got you where you are today. We were all once immature and ignorant, like the prodigal son in Luke 15 who wasted his inheritance on wild living. But the only way to live the life God designed for you is to exchange unproductive, childish paradigms for new fruitful, adult strategies (1 Cor. 13:11).

Sometimes we look back on decisions we've made and think, "If I had known back then what I know now, I would have done things differently." This concept is often referred to as the law of unintended consequence—we make decisions not fully realizing the potential consequence. But this law is not the real reason we are where we are in life—our paradigms are. Because of our mind-sets and the decisions they cause us to make, we allow people, circumstances, our cultures and environments to eat our purpose, sensibilities, and destinies for breakfast, lunch, and dinner. And we reap the unwanted results again and again. The prodigal son did this. He left his father's house and wasted his inheritance in a foreign land, surrounded by people who made it their mission to take what he had.

But after finding himself surrounded by pigs and scrounging for food, the prodigal son "came to himself" and decided to return to his father's house (Luke 15:17). The Bible calls this act repentance, and it always begins with a paradigm shift. The prodigal son's physical and emotional transformation began with a change in his mind-set.

A paradigm is a worldview. It is the mental models, concepts, ideologies, philosophies, and intellectual strongholds we hold in our minds and believe to be true. Paradigms—produced through socialization, education, culturalization, and relational constellations—affect the way we look at life and understand our whole lives.

The paradigms we embrace come from our life experiences. They consist of self-imposed mental rules and regulations concerning how the world works and what we must do or not do to achieve happiness and success in it. They include the stories we tell ourselves and others that affect the roles that we play in life.

To further explain a paradigm let's use the example of a computer. The mind is like the hardware and a paradigm is like the software. Once installed in the mind, paradigms drive our responses and reactions, experiences and influence—from the people we meet and with whom we subsequently form relationships to the events and situations that occur in our lives.

√ Paradigms affect our reception of information and stimuli on a daily basis by acting as filters through which we see the world. They sift and bend incoming information to fit the self-imposed rules of our paradigms. That filtered information then becomes an integral part of our belief system.

The paradigms we hold are representational truths. They underscore what we already believe and shield us from what we do not believe. They are essentially the perceptual glasses we wear in order to "see" the realities in our world. In other words, paradigms affect how we perceive things.

> " The paradigms we hold are representational truths. They underscore what we already believe and shield us from what we do not believe. "

Over the years we become comfortable with our paradigms and so we trust them. We believe our paradigms are "right" and therefore when challenged by the possibilities of something new, we attempt to protect ourselves by employing defense mechanisms. These defense mechanisms are subconscious mental tactics developed over time that protect us from impulses and feelings such as anxiety and fear that are too difficult for the conscious mind to face. For example, if you are faced with a particularly unpleasant task, your mind may choose to forget your responsibility in order to avoid the dreaded assignment. In addition to forgetting, other defense mechanisms include rationalization, denial, repression, projection, and rejection.

The problem with every paradigm we hold is this: if the principle, pattern, or model on which it is based is in error, the paradigm will cause us to live a life of errors. Since a paradigm gives us a context for processing information, if the context is wrong or faulty, the conclusion will be wrong or faulty.

Our old context was the kingdom of darkness. Because God has delivered us from the kingdom of darkness and brought us into the kingdom of light, it behooves us to remember that the kingdom of darkness is built on error, deception, and lies. And as long as we hold on to our current mind-sets based on that dark kingdom, we will always be led astray.

A paradigm can distort what is false and make it appear true, or it can distort what is true and make it appear false. Both will lead us to deception. That is why the message of the kingdom is powerful. It has the divine power to shift paradigms and transform minds through its concepts.

Unfortunately our paradigms are not easily altered. Sometimes it takes a crisis—or a series of crises—to chisel away at the core of these cultural constructs, religious strongholds, repressed residue, and psychological stratifications.

When people cry out for help, it is usually because their negative emotional patterns have become too painful for them to tolerate or because their entire world seems to be falling apart. This period of disintegration or disorientation is part of the process of stepping from the old into the new. Isaac Newton's law of motion says a body at rest tends to stay at rest unless an external force moves it. Your soul wants to stay at rest, but the Spirit of the Lord wants to renew your mind and shift your paradigms out of their state of rest. God sends His truth to penetrate deeply and adjust your paradigms so they are aligned with His Word. Embracing that truth is where change begins.

> A paradigm can distort what is false and make it appear true, or it can distort what is true and make it appear false.

In Luke 8:22–25 the disciples are trying to shift from one part of the country to another. They were traveling in a boat, and while they were en route a storm came that caused them to fear for their lives. But when the disciples cried out to Him, Jesus rebuked the storm, and immediately the wind and the waves calmed. The storm the disciples faced was divinely staged and sovereignly allowed so that their thoughts would be altered dimensionally. They experienced a true paradigm shift when they came to realize that even a raging storm was no match for Jesus.

You may be going through a storm right now. It may be a physical storm, an emotional storm, or a financial storm. Adverse winds of confusion may have blown into your marriage, wrecked your business, or destroyed your faith in God. But there is hope. Your storms are no match for Jesus. David said:

> I cried out to the LORD, and he answered me from his holy mountain. I lay down and slept, yet I woke up in safety, for the LORD was watching over me. I am not afraid of ten thousand enemies who surround me on every side.
>
> Arise, O LORD! Rescue me, my God! Slap all my enemies in the face! Shatter the teeth of the wicked! Victory comes from you, O LORD. May you bless your people.
>
> —PSALM 3:4–7, NLT

God is still able to speak peace into any storm—even if we brought it upon ourselves! In the parable of the prodigal son, we see a vivid illustration of the grace of God at work. The father in the story represents God, who graciously welcomes us to Himself no matter our faults or failures. The prodigal son represents the believer who embraces the Father's grace, which is made available to each of us through repentance. Because of grace you can change. Because of grace you can live life on purpose and abide in the realm of power, authority, and dominion.

Because of God's grace you don't have to wallow in a state you were not wired to live in. You can break the emotional and mental chains that keep you bound in situations you desire to be liberated from the moment you have the courage and audacity to shift your way of thinking and proclaim, "I deserve to live better and to be treated better!"

THE PIGPEN

Years ago I watched a video that explored how people change. It exposed the fact that many individuals were not willing or able to change ingrained habits and thought patterns until they experienced a "significant emotional event." These events are the defining moments in our lives. One such moment happened to Saul on the road to Damascus, when he was knocked off his horse and rendered blind for three days. God closed his natural eyes so that he could have an eye-opening spiritual experience.

The pain you are experiencing may become the very thing that helps you find the motivation to change. The struggling, depression, constant anxiety, and smoldering hostility you feel may be the catalyst that brings you to your defining moment—your aha moment—just as in the story of the prodigal son. His defining moment came in a pigpen when he had hit rock bottom in life. It was the moment when he became aware and appreciative of the fact that the course he was on would undermine his potential, worth, and dignity, thus leading him to a sad nowhere.

Scripture is littered with examples of people who came to places where they faced defining moments:

- For Abraham, it was Ur of Chaldea, where he decided to leave the known and follow God to a land He would show him (Gen. 12).

- For Moses, it was a desert where he was called to liberate his people (Exod. 3).

- For the children of Israel, it was Goshen, where God supernaturally protected them (Exod. 9:22–26).

- For Jacob, it was Jabbok, where his name was changed after he wrestled with God and was transformed (Gen. 32:22–32).

- For Isaac, it was the Valley of Gerar, where he experienced economic breakthrough (Gen. 26:17–25).

- For Elijah, it was the brook Cherith, where God provided food and water for him during a time of drought (1 Kings 17:1–7).

- For Elisha, it was Bethel, a place challenged by the prophetic conditions, where Elisha was tested for ministry (2 Kings 2:23–24).

- For David, it was the Cave of Adullam, a place for the socially outcast where David was developed into a leader (1 Sam. 22:1–5).

- For Joshua, it was Jericho, a place of strategic warfare (Josh. 6:1–27).

- For Paul, it was the Damascus Road, where he was confronted by God and converted (Acts 9:1–8).

- For Peter, it was the sea, his place of transition into dominion (Matt. 14:28–30).

- For Jesus, it was Golgotha, the place of His crucifixion (John 19).

For the prodigal son, the pigpen was the place of transformation, where his true identity was restored. Every one of us has prophetic pigpen experiences. These are the places where we face the defining moments in our lives and grace helps us to replace our childhood scripts with adult strategies and begin to live the life God planned for us.

Change, however, isn't easy. Coming to these defining moments can lead to feelings of confusion and conflict, because two controlling systems are attempting to occupy (or dominate) the same mental space or control the same emotional resources. Psychologists call this a "limbo of chaos and uncertainty."

Two forces are vying for the same space in your head, creating a "do I or don't I" mental tug-of-war. It's like when two individuals are fighting to possess the television remote control. As long as one has the control of the remote, the other will fight

> " Every one of us has prophetic pigpen experiences...where we face the defining moments in our lives. "

in an attempt to gain possession. This is what happens in your mind on a daily basis as you choose to serve God.

To overcome this confusion and internal conflict, you must take action. Action breaks confusion because you are no longer being pulled between two opinions—you have made a decision.

William T. Powers, a control systems theorist and author of *Making Sense of Behavior: The Meaning of Control*, said, "Behavior is the control of perception."[6] You can control your perception by digging into God's Word to see what He says about you. Writer Anaïs Nin is quoted as saying, "We don't see things as they are, we see things as we are."[7] See yourself the way God sees you and from that perspective begin to take action by faith.

Seek God for His plans and purposes for your future and move in that direction. If you don't take deliberate steps toward a goal, you will never reach it. Human beings are not omniscient. We do not always have all the facts and information we need to make decisions. In the absence of sufficient information, our minds simulate different scenarios and courses of action. The brain goes into its databank of memories and automatically fills in the missing pieces by interpreting what we sense via the mental models we have stored in our memories.

This capacity to fill in the blanks happens in every aspect of life. It happens economically, relationally, spiritually, and so on. For instance, when you are driving on the highway, your peripheral view is fraught with blind spots, but your brain automatically takes in all the surrounding information and seamlessly connects the dots, creating the appearance of a solid field of vision. Likewise, the human brain constantly relies on prior patterns to interpret situations in the absence of information. We call these patterns mental models.

As long as you don't have a vision for your future, your mind will fill in the blanks with experiences from your past. If you do this for so long, even unconsciously, your future will become an exact replica of your past. Stop repeating the stories of your past by allowing God to change your paradigms.

At the beginning of His earthly ministry, Jesus introduced a new paradigm. He preached, "Repent, for the kingdom of heaven is at hand" (Matt. 4:17). Repentance is the catalyst that brings about true change, because change begins in the mind, and repentance begins with a paradigm shift. When you change the way you think, you change the way you live.

Life happens in a series of moments. There are twenty thousand moments in a day. Those moments create momentum, and momentum creates monuments. The pigpen became a monumental experience for the prodigal son because it helped him find his way home.

No matter what you have faced, regardless of what you have been through, you don't have to feel as if you are an outcast. You can find your way back to our heavenly Father's arms—today. Your future comes to you minute by minute by minute. Each moment announces an opportunity for something new to happen. Your task is to recognize your destiny moment and seize it.

Your future is for sale. Don't mortgage it. Buy it by owning the moment.

You are writing the story of your life, one moment at a time. Make certain it is epic.

The philosopher Horace said, "There is a critical minute for all things."[8] How you respond to these moments will determine the course of your life and the nature of your destiny. You can procrastinate or bellyache about everything that is wrong or you can make a decision to do something different and do it now. You can be distracted and lose precious moments or you can focus on what you want rather than on what you do not want.

Stop procrastinating. Procrastinators and those who lack focus tend to let opportunities slip. They put off until tomorrow what they should do today. Don't procrastinate. Don't let one more opportunity pass you by because you did not capture that moment.

David said, "So teach us to number our days, that we may gain a heart of wisdom" (Ps. 90:12).

Now is the only moment you have to seize everything you ever wanted.

This moment.

Not tomorrow.

Not later, but now.

The defining moments of our lives are not
determined by the evil done to us, but by our
response through the grace and power of God.[9]

—DAVID C. MCCASLAND

CHAPTER 3

BREAKING THE TIES
THAT BIND

*There are two primary choices in life: to accept conditions as
they exist, or accept the responsibility for changing them.*[1]
—DENIS WAITLEY

THE CHOICES WE make create the world in which we
live. This truth is both sobering and liberating. On
one hand it means you cannot blame others for your
predicaments. Any problem is, at the very least, a joint
effort between circumstances, other people, and your
own decisions. The liberating part is that if you perceive the reality in your world one way, you can choose
to change your perception and stop being a victim of
circumstances.

If you blame others for your present state and fail to
take responsibility for what is going on in your world,
you render yourself powerless. Society encourages this
way of thinking. We have been programmed to make
such statements as, "You bore me," which is translated,
"You make me feel bored." Or we say, "You make me
sick," which means, "You make me feel sick." Giving
other people control over your emotional states is so

easy to do with your language. You decree a thing and it is established. If you say a thing so often, your life can become a self-fulfilled prophecy. Change your thoughts and speech and you will change your life.

Change and transformation begin in the mind! Scripture says, "Don't copy the behavior and customs of this world, but let God transform you into a new person by changing the way you think. Then you will learn to know God's will for you, which is good and pleasing and perfect" (Rom. 12:2, NLT). And, "Let this mind be in you which was also in Christ Jesus" (Phil. 2:5).

People who have hurt or offended us often become the focal point of our daily activities. But as we discussed in the previous chapter, you can rewire your mind and retrain your thinking. This is the best way to begin to give yourself a new beginning. What you focus on affects every part of your being. So fill your mind with the Word of God and receive its liberating truth about who you are and God's plans for your life.

Many of us live tormented lives because we rehearse the horrible things that have happened to us. We are not able to forgive and forget. Forgiving those who have hurt, abused, or abandoned us is the most beautiful thing we can do for ourselves, our friends, our families, those we love, and even our communities and nations.

Change your speech and you will change your life.

Painful experiences have the ability to create negativity that eventually poisons the soul and spirit, spilling out like an acid that corrodes everything and everyone attached to us. Instead of forgiving ourselves and others for the mistakes and missteps made, we become filled with bitterness and hatred. We talk about "hating" our lives. Ann Landers is quoted as saying, "Hate, like acid, does more damage to the vessel in which it is stored than to the object on which it is poured."[2] Forgiveness neutralizes that acid and empowers us to become whole.

When you forgive and forget, you don't disregard the negative occurrence. To forget simply means that you no longer let it have power over your present life, your future success, your progress, or your prosperity. It means that you give yourself permission to not only change your life story but also to secure a new life script created by new paradigms. These new paradigms are created through the knowledge of Scripture, which contains wisdom keys and practical principles for living. To build new paradigms you must think on "what is true, and honorable, and right, and pure, and lovely, and admirable. Think about things that are excellent and worthy of praise. Keep putting into practice all you learned and received from me—everything you heard from me and saw me doing. Then the God of peace will be with you" (Phil. 4:8–9, NLT).

Mastery in your life starts with mastery of your thoughts, which is tantamount to self-discipline. If you don't control what you think, you can't control what you do and who you become. (See Philippians 4:8–9.) You do not need to be a product of your environment or imprisoned by circumstances. Self-discipline enables you to control your thoughts so that you control your destiny.

> **Spiritual growth is determined by how much your soul has been changed by the Word of God.**

If you want to change your life, maintain perspective. Keep the main thing the main thing. Do not play the blame game. Take personal responsibility for your thoughts, feelings, and actions. Learn to say I am sorry and do not take your frustrations and anger out on those you love. Guard against displacing and transferring your emotions and fight negativity because it will further entrench you into bondage—mentally, spiritually, and emotionally. Your enemy is not your children, employees, parents, friends, or spouse—so don't lash out. They don't deserve to be the object of your pain.

Stop trying to fix things and people. Let the Word of God penetrate your soul like a laser. Meditate on the Word day and night "that you may observe to do according to all that is written in it. For then you will make your way prosperous, and then you will have good success" (Josh. 1:8).

CHANGED FROM THE INSIDE OUT

No matter where you go and what you go through, God is with you. He will never leave you or forsake you. It's all right to cry, because God will wipe the tears from your eyes (Isa. 25:8; Rev. 21:4). You may have been handed a bad deal from the day you were born and endured some lousy circumstances, but I am here to tell you that does not have be your final epitaph! As a believer, Christ has made you free. You must engage that freedom.

Christianity is not just another religion. It is the life of God abiding within and flowing through you. The wonderful thing about this life source is that it will completely transform you from the inside out. When you are born again, your spirit is instantly transformed into the image of God. The spirit is that part of you that takes on the nature of God. According to Scripture, when you are born again you should immediately start the process of "renewing your mind." Your mind is housed in your soul along with your will and emotions. Spiritual growth is determined by how much your soul has been changed by the Word of God.

James 1:21 states, "Wherefore lay apart all filthiness and superfluity of naughtiness, and receive with meekness the engrafted word, which is able to save your souls" (KJV). There is nothing wrong with your spirit if you are born again; the life of God is in there. The Holy Spirit dwells within you. What hinders you from living a spiritual life is having a soul (mind) that thinks like the world instead of like God. This is true because your soul (will) also determines your actions. Your body is just your "earth suit."

Once you have been born again, the Bible instructs you to "put on the new man, which after God is created in righteousness and true holiness" (Eph. 4:24, KJV).

This means your soul and body are to take on the same image as your spirit. This happens through the process of changing your mind, your will, and your emotions to understand and walk in the ways of God.

Who you are today has been shaped by the decisions you made yesterday. All of your decisions are shaped by what I call the Core 8 Human drives:

1. The drive to bond
2. The drive to be known
3. The drive to know
4. The drive to grow
5. The drive to acquire
6. The drive to accomplish
7. The drive for significance
8. The drive for safety

Why is this important for you to know? Because then you will be able to peer beneath the surface of your problem to understand what is driving your behaviors. Drives are like appetites—they must be satisfied. Many people have chosen illegitimate and even illegal ways of satisfying these drives. In so doing they have formed uncontrollable and insatiable habits, lusts, and addictions.

When these drives are not brought under the lordship of Christ, they will cause you to lose control of your soul and form unhealthy attachments in an attempt to satisfy your longings. This is what happened to the prodigal son. His drives were not bad; it was the way he attempted to satisfy them that led to his self-destructive behavior. He attached himself to people who did not have his spiritual DNA nor the capacity to discern his true potential and ability. As a result, they essentially belittled his worth as a human being.

The Bible cautions against attaching yourself to the wrong people:

> Be ye not unequally yoked together with unbelievers: for what fellowship hath righteousness with unrighteousness? And what communion hath light with darkness? And what concord hath Christ with Belial? Or what part hath he that believeth with an infidel? And what agreement hath the temple of God with idols? For ye are the temple of the living God; as God hath said, I will dwell in them, and walk in them; and I will be their God, and they shall be my people. Wherefore come out from among them, and be ye separate, saith the Lord, and touch not the unclean thing; and I will receive you, And will be a Father unto you, and ye shall be my sons and daughters, saith the Lord Almighty.
>
> —2 CORINTHIANS 6:14–18, KJV

While attachments can be healthy and legitimate, such as the ones you develop with your spouse, parents, or friends, they can also be harmful, as in the case of the prodigal son. Attachments become the catalyst for the decisions you make on a day-to-day basis. They become the glue that holds together your mental models; which determine how you function and see yourself in the world. Author and architect Richard Buckminster Fuller is often quoted as saying, "You never change things by fighting the existing reality. To change something, build a new model that makes the existing model obsolete."[3] It could very well be that if Henry Ford had asked people what they wanted, they might have told him a faster horse and buggy.

In Hebrews 8:13 we read that God has established a new covenant, making the first "old." This verse speaks to the law of displacement. You cannot remove that which is old until there is something new. Allowing God to give you a new paradigm will ensure the old is removed.

Refuse to be tempted to do the same thing over and over expecting a different result. Do the same, remain the same. Do different; live different. Could things be the way they are because you are the way you are? What one thing can you change that can change everything? You can change how you relate to and bond with people, things, and situations. You can change old habits when you embrace new ones.

CUTTING UNHEALTHY TIES

The connections you make are important. We were created to bond. But being bonded to relationships that are toxic, abusive, and sabotaging undermines our purpose, progress, dignity, and self-worth. When we find ourselves in toxic relationships that we can't seem to escape, that is often a sign that there are soul ties in our lives that need to be broken.

Soul ties are spiritual, emotional, and psychological attachments to things, people, and experiences that, at a subconscious level, influence decisions we make in life. They are predominantly created through close relationships with individuals or groups of people that entrench us in particular conditions. Soul ties are a major contributor to the occurrence of negative cycles in an individual's life. Unhealthy ties contaminate, control, and deform the human spirit, causing emotional toxicity. Time, distance, distraction, and even death do not automatically cancel or eradicate these deeply rooted ties.

The less you associate with some people, the more your life will improve. Mediocrity in others increases mediocrity in you. Successful people are impatient with negative thinking and negative people. Negative people do not add to your life; they only make withdrawals.

As you grow and mature, your associates will change. Some of your friends will not want to progress, and they will want you to stay where they are. Instead of helping you climb they will want you to crawl. Your friends will either add to your life or take away from it. They will either expand your vision or choke your dream, so examine what and to whom you are attached.

Remember this: never receive counsel from unproductive people. Never share your problems with unproductive people, because those who aren't moving forward themselves will not be able to tell you how to move past your problem. You are certain to be on the worse end of the bargain when you exchange ideas with an unproductive person.

Don't follow anyone who isn't going anywhere. Some people you spend an evening with; in others you invest your time and resources.

Wise is the person who fortifies his life with the right friendships. If you run with wolves, you will learn to howl. If you associate with eagles, you will soar to great heights. "A mirror reflects a man's face, but what he is really like is shown by the kind of friends he chooses" (Prov. 27:19, TLB).

To examine your relationships and determine which ones are healthy enough to keep, ask yourself what value the individual brings to your life. Does the person aid in your growth and development? Every person you associate with should add value to your life somehow. So ask yourself: "Does this person have the capacity for me?" "Do I know what I want from him?" "Does she know what she needs from me?" "Can he add value to me?" "Can I add value to him?" Your relationships should be mutually beneficial. Get rid of the leeches and parasites—people who draw from you and give nothing in return.

Some soul ties are created through the attachments we form. Other types of soul ties are created through vows, commitments, agreements, and other exchanges of words. You may be completely unaware of the agreements you made in the spiritual realm when you said, "Over my dead body," or "So and so makes me sick," or

"If such and such doesn't happen I will die," or "This is to die for." But your words bind you to an outcome—they tie your soul to a future event.

The spoken word creates frequencies, or vibrations and waves. It is like they build an invisible track. Your words travel on a specific frequency and are transmitted back to you manifested as an experience or occurrence in your life. Words create a kind of magnetism in the realm of the spirit. Though invisible, they are very real. Your words provide a kind of spiritual homing device that attracts either positive people, things, and experiences or negative people, things, and experiences. I explore this concept in great detail in my book *Commanding Your Morning*, because understanding the power of your words is a life-changing revelation.

Think about this: How many times this week did you talk about how badly you have been hurt or how you have been wronged? How many times a day do you think about a past hurt? Has it become a stake driven into the soil of your memories that prevents you from moving away from those hurts? If so, your future is anchored to your past. You will be able to move only so far but no further, almost as if some invisible puppeteer is controlling your every action.

You can stop being a victim and reclaim your power as soon as you decide that you want to change. You can break the ties that bind you when you get sick and tired of being sick and tired. When have hit your personal rock bottom and are ready to rebound. When you are willing to take the risk associated with thinking and acting in new ways. When you take responsibility for how you feel and how you perceive yourself in relation to people around you. When you change the way you look at things and people. This is when you're ready to change.

If you're reading this book and thinking to yourself, "I have already fallen apart quite badly," I want to encourage you. If you are willing to expend the energy, with God's help you can put the pieces of your life back together again—but in a new and different pattern.

True change begins in the mind. When you change the way you think, you change the way you live. "Change the way I think about what?" you may ask. Change the way you think about your life, your past, your hurt, your pain, the perpetrator or violator. Change the way you think about anything that contradicts what the Word of God says. When you choose to change, you will find the power to end bad habits, break unhealthy ties, and create the bright and prosperous future God designed for you.

> Don't copy the behavior and customs of this world, but let God transform you into a new person by changing the way you think. Then you will learn to know God's will for you, which is good and pleasing and perfect.
> —ROMANS 12:2, NLT

CHAPTER 4

HEALING THE PAIN
OF GUILT AND SHAME

Instead of their shame my people will receive a double
portion, and instead of disgrace they will rejoice in
their inheritance; and so they will inherit a double por-
tion in their land, and everlasting joy will be theirs.
—ISAIAH 61:7, NIV

O VERCOMING IS AN ongoing process that requires personal integrity, not just for some of us but for all of us. I have been hurt deeply, but I also have hurt. I have been disappointed, but I have also disappointed. I have made many mistakes. I, like everyone else, am still under construction.

Here is the bad news: we have all been both victim and perpetrator. But here is the good news: we are all overcomers. The definition of overcome is incredible. It means to get the better of or gain superiority over difficulties. In other words, no matter what you have been through or what you have done, you do not have to live in defeat because the Bible says you have already overcome by the blood of the Lamb (Rev. 12:11).

Life throws us many curveballs. It's almost as if our

progress is booby-trapped. Depending on the intensity of the situation, there will probably be days when we have to will ourselves to keep moving. The greatest challenge is to muster the inner strength to persevere through difficulties when the stakes are high and our emotional resources are low. Those are the days when you will prove to yourself that you're not a quitter—because you will find the resolve to persist in overcoming the painful events of your past. In your weakness God's strength will be made perfect (2 Cor. 12:9).

These painful events exist in your memory, and those memories give rise to the feelings and thoughts you have about those experiences. No one else lives in this psychological dimension but you. You may choose to share your thoughts and feelings about these past events, and people may attempt to help you to overcome the pain associated with them, but you must do the work of actually overcoming yourself. Like the impotent man in John 5, Jesus will give you the impetus, but you must take up your bed, use your feet, and walk.

Shame is what many people feel when they recall past events. This spirit causes painful emotions—a strong sense of guilt, embarrassment, unworthiness, and disgrace. Individuals who are plagued by the spirit of shame walk through life as emotional puppets. They are easily manipulated and often use manipulative tactics to get people to do what they want. People harassed by shame also struggle with feelings of unworthiness and poor self-image.

The psalmist said, "Because for thy sake I have borne reproach; shame hath covered my face" (Ps. 69:7, KJV). Shame is a master spirit in that it consumes our entire lives. It produces an internal feeling that we are grossly and unbearably flawed as a person. It seduces us into believing that we are inadequate and no good. These feelings impede the maximization of potential and the fulfillment of purpose.

Many people grow up in shame-based homes and communities. Shame can be rooted in family secrets or personal failures that leave us with a poor sense of self. It can stem from self-inflicted conditions such as alcoholism and addictions; from lying, cheating, abortion, murder, or poor performance; or from wrongs perpetrated against us such as human trafficking or verbal or physical abuse. Shame erodes our authenticity, integrity, and credibility, and brings with it a sense of worthlessness, meaninglessness, depression, compulsive disorders, a deep sense of inferiority, inadequacy, alienation, helplessness, victimization, and isolation.

We can feel ashamed about things that happen to us or things that we have done. We all make mistakes. Making mistakes, of course, is a necessary part of progress, innovation, and growth. If you want to succeed and become great, you must risk making mistakes and learn how to leverage them when you do. You have to see every failure as one more step toward your ultimate success. Successful people start where those who fail give up.

Many times we are so paralyzed by shame that we

"hide" our faces—we are stripped of our true self, personality, and identity, and take on a persona other than who we really are. Simply stated, we lose touch with our authenticity as we put on social masks to conceal the real pain emanating from our hearts.

Although they may plague us with the feelings of disgrace, embarrassment, and self-consciousness, no matter how horrendous the precipitating events were in and of themselves, they take on color once you place judgments on them. This color is based on your perception of how deeply the events affected you. This judgment causes you to assign a value that the event is either "good" or "bad," negative or positive, beneficial or harmful. The emotions you experience will correspond to your judgment of the event. So it is not just the pain associated with the actual incident that causes you to become shame-ridden, it is the feelings that result from those judgments that affect you the most.

As the memories replay in our minds as vividly as a movie—live and in Technicolor with 4-D effects—they create states of unhappiness, depression, discouragement, and despondency. This often leads us to throw in the proverbial towel and resign ourselves to live in neutral; imprisoned by our shame. We may never speak of the incident, but like a shaken bottle of soda, the moment we are opened to explore our true feelings, repressed emotions bubble up with profuse force.

There is another pain that is filed away at a subconscious level, far away from our conscious mind. This pain is fear and anxiety. It revisits us in our dream state, causing nightmares, and in our awake state causes irrational phobias, as in the tragic drama of some Shakespearean play. Many people today take medication to rid themselves of the feelings that cause anxiety; they want a way off the roller coaster of apprehensive uneasiness that puts them in a state of distress concerning real or imagined future possibilities, probabilities, or eventualities. This anxious state creates a kind of psychological effect that, when not counteracted by faith in God, will invite fear, hopelessness, depression, worry, and dread to become the prison wardens that put both the present and future on lockdown. But no one has to remain in the jailhouse of torment.

Scripture says, "Be anxious for nothing, but in everything by prayer and supplication, with thanksgiving, let your requests be made known to God" (Phil. 4:6). If you are being plagued by tormenting anxiety, write down your prayer

> Your past wounds can become your future wisdom the moment you recognize that God is at work in you, causing everything to work together for good.

requests in a journal. Then thank God in advance for meeting those needs. Everything can be changed through prayer. If you want to grow in the discipline of prayer, I encourage you to check out my books *The Prayer Warrior's Way* and *'Til Heaven Invades Earth*. They will give you tools and strategies to build a more dynamic and effectual prayer life.

YESTERDAY'S WOUNDS ARE TOMORROW'S WISDOM

Although you can't change the past or wish painful occurrences away, you can decide whether to allow those events to harm you or help you. When the Bible encourages us to forget things that are behind us (Phil. 3:13), I believe God is instructing us to disconnect from the emotional pain associated with the event. We can do this by finding a way to create value out of events we judged as harmful. Joseph did it with his brothers. He said, "As for you, ye thought evil against me; but God meant it unto good, to bring to pass, as it is this day, to save much people alive" (Gen. 50:20, KJV).

Your past wounds can become your future wisdom the moment you recognize that God is at work in you (Phil. 2:13), causing everything to work together for good (Rom. 8:28). Once you realize that you do not have to involve yourself in shadow boxing or live as a tragic puppet whose fragile stage collapses under the weight of guilt and shame, you will be able to embrace past events as springboards for growth by reinterpreting them as positive life lessons that perhaps you can use to help others in their journey toward healing. Even if an event was traumatic, if you will view it as something that can actually be beneficial for your development, you can free yourself from the pain associated with your memory of it.

Remember, difficulties do not spring into existence arbitrarily and accidentally; there is always a cause for every effect. Hurting people hurt people; the perpetrator was once the perpetrated. You can break the cycle by saying, "The buck stops here, right now—today." Refuse to be a victim and take back your life! (See Matthew 11:12.) The spiritual, emotional, and psychological gift of triumphing in (2 Cor. 2:14) and prevailing over (3 John 2) perceived obstacles and setbacks is priceless.

Neither your past nor your current state of affairs has come to pass to destroy you or to cause duress, but to reveal the true strength of your character, the uniqueness of your identity, the importance of your giftedness, the urgency of honing your skills, the relevance of your life, the dignity within your humanity, and the responsibility of discharging your duties and assignments. These truths are worth repeating over and over again until they are nestled in your subconscious mind. And while you are on the path to freedom, there is no need to be ashamed of the tears that will inevitably come. Your tears testify of the courage needed to endure hardship today while resisting the temptation to lose hope for a better tomorrow. Take comfort in the fact that you have been divinely empowered to endure the pain that comes as you pursue a better future.

Do not shy away from the challenge of facing yesterday's wounds. Do not be fearful to grow past the pain. Draw from the strength that comes from living your life in Christ Jesus (Rom. 5:20–21; Rom. 8:2) and rely on the power of the Holy Spirit, who is the greatest empowerment specialist (Isa. 11:2–3). He will give you the wisdom to persevere and the courage to change!

The Bible says:

> Beside this, giving all diligence, add to your faith virtue; and to virtue knowledge; and to knowledge temperance; and to temperance patience; and to patience godliness; and to godliness brotherly kindness; and to brotherly kindness charity. For if these things be in you, and abound, they make you that ye shall neither be barren nor unfruitful in the knowledge of our Lord Jesus Christ. But he that lacketh these things is blind, and cannot see afar off, and hath forgotten that he was purged from his old sins. Wherefore the rather, brethren, give diligence to make your calling and election sure: for if ye do these things, ye shall never fall.
> —2 PETER 1:5–10, KJV

This spiritual exercise is the recipe you need to secure your success, promotions, and prosperity! By building the disciplines of faith, wisdom, patience, perseverance, and so on, your life will be blessed and fruitful!

GET GOD'S PERSPECTIVE

If you have a hard time seeing past the shame of your mistakes or the hurt someone caused you, ask God to give you His perspective, because it will certainly be different from yours. As the Scriptures say:

> Seek the LORD while He may be found,
> Call upon Him while He is near.
> Let the wicked forsake his way,
> And the unrighteous man his thoughts;
> And let him return to the LORD,
> And He will have mercy on him;
> And to our God,
> For He will abundantly pardon.
> "For My thoughts are not your thoughts,
> Nor are your ways My ways," says the LORD.
>
> —ISAIAH 55:6–8

If you ask, God will give you His mind. He will heal your soul and deliver you from all of your afflictions. If you have fallen, God will lift you up (James 4:10). Take responsibility for where you are by asking God for wisdom, and He will generously give it (James 1:5)—for He has given you His Holy Spirit to lead you into all truth (John 16:13). There is no good thing He will withhold from you if you but ask Him (Luke 11:13).

We have all heard of the phrase "mind over matter." John Irving, a novelist and Academy Award–winning screenwriter, once wrote, "Your memory is a monster;

> " God can perform psychological and emotional laser surgery with His Word. "

you forget—it doesn't. It simply files things away. It keeps things for you or hides things from you—and summons them to your recall with a will of its own. You think you have a memory, but it has you."[1]

Many times we are weakened by anxiety (the fear of the unknown). Sometimes we are paralyzed by fear (the knowledge of the known). These are the activities of the mind. If you can change your mind, you can change your life.

Change is tantamount to growth, progress, and healing. Change, however, is easier said than done. Take for instance forgiveness. Maybe someone hurt you. You know the best course of action for healing, growth, and success is to release them, yet you still cannot find the inner strength to do so. Sometimes the pain can be so great you find ways to justify your bitterness and hatred even though Scripture tells us to forgive (Matt. 6:15). Or perhaps the shoe is on the other foot. Maybe you hurt someone else. Maybe you made a choice out of weakness, ignorance, fear, or anger that you now regret and you still feel the shame. Maybe someone resents you or feels intense hatred or bitterness toward you because of your past actions. You don't have to waste time wishing you could go back in time to change what happened. You only need to find a way to turn that hurt or regret into a catalyst for growth and move forward starting today.

Instead of seeing a painful trauma you would rather not think about, you can begin to see an opportunity to ask for forgiveness, receive forgiveness, and use your testimony to minister to others. If a wrong has been perpetrated against you, allow God to touch those tender spots and apply the healing elixir of His love. Allow truth to set you free.

The pain of past events exists nowhere except in the deep recesses of your mind. Deep-seated melancholy can be displaced as you allow the Word of God to penetrate those areas; God can perform psychological and emotional laser surgery with His Word. (See Hebrews 4:12.)

GUILT VS. SHAME

While they are similar emotions, there is a difference between shame and guilt. Guilt is caused when a particular principle is violated or a law broken, but shame is something deeper. Guilt is an emotion. Shame is a state of being. We tend to feel guilty when we have not lived up to expectations and standards that we have set for ourselves. But if we believe that we "should" have behaved differently or we "ought" to have done better, we likely will feel shame.

Although genuine guilt is a healthy emotion, Satan can pervert it by turning it from a remorseful awareness of having done something wrong to self-reproach. When this happens, we know that Satan has perverted a healthy emotion into a deadly weapon. When guilt assails you, rather than wallowing in it to the point of defeat, pray a prayer similar to Psalm 51:1–12, which I quote in part below:

> Have mercy upon me, O God, according to Your lovingkindness; according to the multitude of Your tender mercies, blot out my transgressions. Wash me thoroughly from my iniquity, and cleanse me from my sin. For I acknowledge my transgressions....Create in me a clean heart, O God, and renew a steadfast spirit within me. Do not cast me away from Your presence, and do not take Your Holy Spirit from me. Restore to me the joy of Your salvation, and uphold me by Your generous Spirit.

Remember, overcoming guilt and shame does not mean not caring about your actions. It involves taking responsibility for what you did and coming to terms with it. The key to moving past guilt and shame is in choosing to forgive yourself and others (a theme interwoven throughout this book), and in embracing the fact that God does not want you to walk around under the bondage of condemnation.

We have all experienced some level of joy and happiness, and we have all experienced great pain. The enemy has used the intimate relationships, caring communion, authoritative agreements, binding covenants, deep fellowship, and lasting bonds that God meant for human good and His glory as tools for enslavement and destruction.

David, lamenting the deep emotional pain he experienced from the betrayal of his closest confident Ahithophel, said:

Day and night they go about it upon the walls thereof: mischief also and sorrow are in the midst of it. Wickedness is in the midst thereof: deceit and guile depart not from her streets. For it was not an enemy that reproached me; then I could have borne it: neither was it he that hated me that did magnify himself against me; then I would have hid myself from him: But it was thou, a man mine equal, my guide, and mine acquaintance. We took sweet counsel together, and walked unto the house of God in company. Let death seize upon them, and let them go down quick into hell: for wickedness is in their dwellings, and among them.

As for me, I will call upon God; and the LORD shall save me. Evening, and morning, and at noon, will I pray, and cry aloud: and he shall hear my voice. He hath delivered my soul in peace from the battle that was against me: for there were many with me. God shall hear, and afflict them, even he that abideth of old. Selah. Because they have no changes, therefore they fear not God.

—PSALM 55:10–19, KJV

David, though deeply hurt, managed to put things in perspective. He said they did this because they did not fear God. And he knew where to find solace, peace, and strength—not in another person or a compulsive behavior, but in God. In another Psalm he said:

This poor man cried, and the LORD heard him, and saved him out of all his troubles. The angel of the LORD encampeth round about them that fear him, and delivereth them. O taste and see that the LORD is good: blessed is the man that trusteth in him. O fear the LORD, ye his saints: for there is no want to them that fear him. The young lions do lack, and suffer hunger: but they that seek the LORD shall not want any good thing. Come, ye children, hearken unto me: I will teach you the fear of the LORD. What man is he that desireth life, and loveth many days, that he may see good? Keep thy tongue from evil, and thy lips from speaking guile. Depart from evil, and do good; seek peace, and pursue it. The eyes of the LORD are upon the righteous, and his ears are open unto their cry. The face of the LORD is against them that do evil, to cut off the remembrance of them from the earth. The righteous cry, and the LORD heareth, and delivereth them out of all their troubles. The LORD is nigh unto them that are of a broken heart; and saveth such as be of a contrite spirit. Many are the afflictions of the righteous: but the LORD delivereth him out of them all. He keepeth all his bones: not one of them is broken. Evil shall slay the wicked: and they that hate the righteous shall be desolate. The LORD redeemeth the soul of his servants: and none of them that trust in him shall be desolate.

—PSALM 34:6–22, KJV

Let this psalm comfort you as you begin your healing process. David knew the pain of being both the perpetrator of pain (Ps. 51) and victim of someone else's wrongdoing. In both situations he sought refuge in God. We must do the same.

═══════════

Now thanks be to God who always leads us in triumph in Christ, and through us diffuses the fragrance of His knowledge in every place.

—2 CORINTHIANS 2:14

CHAPTER 5

OVERCOMING THE SPIRIT OF AN ORPHAN: REJECTION AND ABANDONMENT

I will not leave you orphans; I will come to you.
—JOHN 14:18

REJECTION, ABUSE, ABANDONMENT, betrayal, and neglect have caused many Christians to believe they are disqualified from finding true, authentic friendships and lasting intimate relationships. Feeling intense loneliness and psychological disconnection from people, many individuals live with what I call the spirit of an orphan.

Current estimates tell us that there are at least 151 million orphans in the world today.[1] These numbers are staggering and increase each time there is a war, a drought, a natural disaster, a pandemic such as AIDS, or any of the other catastrophes that destroy families. In the natural to be an orphan means to be left behind by maternal and paternal caregivers because of death, physical or emotional abandonment, or abuse. Spiritually any person can be considered an orphan. Anything that causes a person to feel alone

56

and emotionally detached can contribute to an individual living as a spiritual orphan. Within our communities and churches we have many leaders, believers, and children who are orphans. They are unable to connect with others, and uncomfortable with building and thriving in a community, despite having both parents alive, living with them under the same roof, and being surrounded by people who genuinely love them.

I believe as Christians we should help address the world orphan crisis. Yet equally important is the spiritual orphan crisis that stems from abandonment. Abandonment is when a person withdraws his presence and support from another person; reneges on his duty, responsibility, or obligation; or betrays covenant or commitment. The enemy seduces people, particularly those who play a key role in another person's development and progress, to renege on commitments and contracts and to walk away from relationships and responsibilities. This act of abdication has the power to cause great emotional pain, financial hardship, spiritual misalignment, organizational chaos, and confusion in the abandoned.

Abandonment can be physical, psychological, or emotional, and can occur with one's job or career, a political or military post, a ministry assignment, and within family relationships. Issues arising from abandonment include the inability to trust, manipulation, shame, fear of rejection, loneliness, suspicion, addictions, codependency, and a host of other maladaptive sets of behavior that interfere with a person's ability to foster future healthy and loving relationships.

I have found that the orphan paradigm often remains even after a person has been adopted. Thus this mindset is more than an emotional and psychological state of being but also a spiritual phenomenon—one that can be broken only when a person fully embraces the fact that God wants to be our heavenly Father who adopts us into His family.

Romans 8 gives us an amazing promise starting in verse 14. The passage reads:

> For as many as are led by the Spirit of God, these are sons [and daughters] of God. For you did not receive the spirit of bondage again to fear, but you received the Spirit of adoption by whom we cry out, "Abba, Father." The Spirit Himself bears witness with our spirit that we are children of God, and if children, then heirs—heirs of God and joint heirs with Christ, if indeed we suffer with Him, that we may also be glorified together.
> —ROMANS 8:14–17

Even if we have experienced abandonment, rejection, or betrayal in any form or fashion, God gives us the spirit of adoption to heal our abandonment issues. We are not alone—there is someone who will fight for us: the God who loves us so dearly and longs for us to call Him "Abba," or "Daddy."

I grew up without a father. It was not until I received

the revelation that I had a heavenly Father who loves me that I was delivered from the orphan spirit. The journey to this understanding—the journey home, as I like to think of it—was long and often dark and lonely. At times I still see little signs that there are areas of trust that still need healing. But in coming to know God, I also came to know that I was His child, and that He unconditionally loved me more than I loved Him, or even myself. The same is true for you—you have someone who unconditionally loves you.

Through my own personal experience, I also came to see the subtle power of the orphan spirit and how it limits our destinies by putting a lid on how connected we are to a community and how open we are to allowing others to know us and to love us. I saw how important it is to break this emotionally isolating condition of psychological detachment by receiving the love from "Daddy God" as my heavenly Father, and I hope you will too.

In these last days I believe the spirit of revival and renewal will be characterized by the spirit of adoption, a period when God will reveal His sincere loving-kindness in a profound way. Love is one of those words that causes so many to cringe because they associate it with individuals who, in a "loving" relationship, hurt them. "God is not a man, that He should lie" (Num. 23:19). Look at how the Old Testament prophet Malachi records the coming move of God:

> Behold, I will send you Elijah the prophet before
> the coming of the great and dreadful day of the

LORD. And he will turn the hearts of the fathers
to the children, and the hearts of the children to
their fathers.

—MALACHI 4:5–6

What I believe he is describing here is the spirit of adoption.

A HARLOT'S SON

We can probably name most of the people in the "hall of faith" of Hebrews chapter 11, but tucked away in verse 32 is Jephthah. "Who?" you may ask. Well, let me tell you his story.

Jephthah's story is told in Judges 11. His father had a fling one night with a prostitute, and Jephthah was the result. Then when his father, Gilead, had other children with his wife and those children came of age, Jephthah's half-siblings chased him out of their home and told him, "You shall have no inheritance in our father's house, for you are the son of another woman" (Judg. 11:2). Enter the orphan spirit. Disinherited, rejected, and wounded in the house of his father, Jephthah fled to become an outlaw.

He set up residence in the land of Tob and there banded together with "worthless men" (Judg. 11:3) who went out raiding with him. He was like David in another skin, who, rejected by his "adoptive" father King Saul, fled when Saul grew jealous of him and tried to kill him, and "everyone who was in distress, everyone who was in debt, and everyone who was discontented gathered to him" (1 Sam. 22:2). These became David's mighty men—his own personal army. Those gathered to Jephthah became a similar band.

When Ammon invaded the land of Jephthah's father, Gilead, the Gileadite elders came to Jephthah for help, knowing he had become a mighty warrior. They told him if he delivered them from the Ammonites,

> 66 At the root of the orphan spirit is bitterness that isolates and then incubates that isolation into all manner of bad things. 99

he could become their leader. It was at this point Jephthah recognized the bitterness of the orphan spirit that was in his heart: "Did you not hate me, and expel me from my father's house? Why have you come to me now when you are in distress?" (Judg. 11:7).

Jephthah had to make a choice: either he would remain bitter and exiled, choosing to identify with the orphan spirit, or he could choose to be redeemed and become the leader he was destined to be. Jephthah chose the spirit of adoption and became a judge of Israel, delivering them from the Ammonites and ruling over them for six years.

Do you see what the orphan spirit does? Although Jephthah was destined for leadership, the orphan spirit turned him into a criminal instead. Disenfranchised, he felt his only option was to fend for himself, reject societal norms, and get ahead by any means he could. At the root of the orphan spirit is bitterness that isolates and then incubates that isolation into all manner of bad things. Feeling rejected and on their own, orphans grab for happiness and fulfillment any way they can, usually compromising for self-promoting, shallow gains rather than what is wholesome and beneficial to all.

A spiritual orphan is one who feels alone; one who feels that he does not have a safe and secure place in healthy, mutually beneficial relationships that affirm, protect, provide, and express love to them. They feel as if they do not belong anywhere. They are driven by fear, anxiety, insecurity, and bitterness—and we know bitterness is a poison that leads to all kinds of strife and dysfunction.

Bitterness begins with a hurt, betrayal, rejection, or offense, and then it progresses through a fairly regular set of phases:

1. Hurt/offense
2. Anger/confusion
3. Resentment
4. Vindictiveness
5. Unforgiveness/indifference
6. Chronic bitterness/stress
7. Stress-related illnesses (such as cancer or arthritis)

Jephthah was an orphan, abandoned by his primary caregiver and his family. Upon his rejection, he fled and had to fend for himself. He must have gone through each of the phases mentioned above. It is likely he became emotionally unavailable, self-centered, indifferent, distrusting, and probably violent. He struck back at a world that had been unkind to him, robbing him of the most fundamental of needs—family. A dysfunctional family led to Jephthah being a dysfunctional person. It was not until he rejected the spirit of being an orphan and embraced his God-ordained destiny that he was able to escape his bitterness and fulfill his potential. His relational skill set was restored, and he became the great man of God he was meant to be.

GOD'S KINGDOM IS A FAMILY

The kingdom of God is based upon relationship, and the central relationship of the kingdom is one of parent to child—father and mother to son and daughter. Look at the language of adoption the apostle Paul used as he spoke about relationships in the church.

> Timothy, a true son in the faith.
>
> —1 TIMOTHY 1:2

> For though you might have ten thousand instructors in Christ, yet you do not have many fathers; for in Christ Jesus I have begotten you through the gospel.
>
> —1 CORINTHIANS 4:15

We become orphaned when those who are caring for us abandon us or when those who should care for us do not. We may have an orphan spirit because of the natural parenting we received. Perhaps you were literally abandoned at birth or your natural parents died. Perhaps you had an absentee father or abusive mother. Perhaps you raised yourself because your parents were always working or you had so many siblings you became a caregiver as soon as you could walk.

On the spiritual side neglect happens at every level of the institutional church. Leaders demand instead of admonish, berate instead of beseech, are busy with church life instead of the inner lives of their people, and are not themselves being parented by a network of caring mentors. Church leaders make promises of parental love, but in reality there is no more attention given than the weekly request for the tithe. Many are hurt by this and leave the church, but we must realize this is not by the spirit of Christ, which is the spirit of adoption. It is another spirit that makes people orphans.

To counteract this trend, we must learn to forgive. Forgiveness is the only way to uproot the weed of bitterness in our lives. Forgiveness is not about the other person; forgiveness is so you can be free from the prison of hatred and self-degradation, from the cancer of the soul and the virus of the mind. It is about shaking free of the emotional bondages that create the "issues in the tissues" that are at the root of sickness and disease. Forgiveness is about opening your heart and living. It is about being freed from emotional numbness and the pain of a shame-based existence. It is about healing your life and relationships.

Forgiveness allows the spirit of adoption to come

into our lives and resurrect our souls from the grave of bitterness, our purposes from the prison of unforgiveness, and our destinies from the destructive force of revenge. It allows us to feel alive and have the freedom to be ourselves, to express ourselves, and to live authentically without feeling that somehow we are unworthy or unlovable. It empowers you to rid yourself of fear and loneliness or the urge to fight or flee. It gives you permission to give love and to receive love—to love unconditionally and to make yourself vulnerable and transparent in the process.

Forgiveness is affirming—it gives you that pat on the back and high five just for acknowledging your deepest need for belonging. It knows that intimacy does not have to find expression through your sexuality. It realizes that harboring a desire for vengeance undermines your success and prosperity. It gives you permission to explore the pain and heal it—whether that is with the help of a friend, a pastor, or a therapist. It is saying no to the familiar state of sadness and yes to gladness.

Jephthah overcame the seduction of the orphan spirit and opened his heart to trust again. Through the love of God and by the power of His Spirit, you too can trust again—even if that trust begins only with God. He will heal your heart and teach you how to trust yourself and then, eventually, how to trust others who are deserving of your trust.

Trust involves opening your heart. Spiritual orphans have closed their hearts because they are afraid of being hurt. They refuse to make themselves vulnerable because of past pains and betrayals. Their spirits are closed to a love relationship with their heavenly Father because they do not trust Him. Instead of running to God, they are continually running away from Him.

They may marry, but they bring with them that dysfunctional mistrust that undermines their family relationships because they do not understand real intimacy. Spiritual orphans are dysfunctional at home and in the workplace because they lack the basic trust needed to have healthy relationships with those in authority. They find themselves battling with fear, control issues, independence, and ego. They are not able to have close relationships because they are not able to receive comfort or love from God or others.

||||||||||||||||||||||||||||||||||||||||||||||||||||||||||||||||||||||||||||||||||||||||||||||||||||

CHARACTERISTICS OF SOMEONE WITH AN ORPHAN SPIRIT

- As children, adolescents, and adults, they idolize others, then quickly devalue and reject them when disappointed.

- They are too angry with others to see their own hurt and fears.

- They are emotionally hypersensitive.

- The live on an emotional roller coaster, swinging from one end of the continuum to the other—from high highs to low lows and back again.

- Their emotions shift quickly. This causes others to walk on eggshells around them.

- Over time they become afraid to hope in others for fear of being disappointed.

- Often they don't trust that relationships will last, so they pick fights, manipulate situations, and sabotage the closeness they fear will inevitably come to an end anyway. With each new separation, their "I can't trust anyone" worldview becomes more fixed.

- They will assault people they grow close to, often in a verbal or physical manner.

- They are good at justifying their actions with rapid-fire reasons for their failure to be a good friend or spouse. Unintentionally they will try to make the other person feel as bad as they do without even recognizing that they feel bad.

- They are vacillators:

  > For the male, vacillator dads often become jealous of their children when a mother's instincts, hormones, and mirror neurons draw them closer together. The dad will become distressed that the passion between him and his wife is lost. The father will then become angry with the mother for abandoning him—even though she hasn't—and may withdraw.

> > For the female, the roller coaster she is on will leave her life and relationships constantly on a spin.

> > When vacillators feel love dying, they may act out and have an affair in an attempt to get their narcissistic needs met by trying to recreate the intensity of the first love—something they erroneously construe as intimacy.

- They see people as either good or bad. "Bad people" are unforgiveable and must be sentenced to life in psychological prison from which "escape" is impossible.

- Forgiveness is a foreign word. This persistent lack of forgiveness and subsequent rumination about the perceived hurt they feel spreads a protective veneer over their vulnerable emotions of fear and sadness.

- They are lone rangers—independent and self-sufficient. They are afraid of asking for help, irrationally believing that people should be able to read their minds or see that they need help. They are convinced that if they were really loved by others, the other person would know what they needed without having to ask.

- They "buy" love.

- They are easily manipulated or use manipulative tactics to get their way.

- They are indifferent in that they refuse to let their feelings get in the way. The can be emotionally unavailable and emotionally detached.

- Conversely, they can have smothering-clingy love.
- They are afraid of being alone or conversely, they are loners.
- They have a challenge connecting on a deep level, especially if it makes them feel vulnerable, inevitably leaving them feeling as if they are not really a part of a larger community of people.
- They have a chip on their shoulders.
- They get communication cues wrong.

||||||||||||||||||||||||||||||||||||||||||||||||||||||||||||||||||||||||||||||||||||||||||||||||||||||||||||||

A spiritual orphan always feels like an "outsider." Even in worship, which requires intimacy with God, there is a tendency to remain in the "outer court" of God's presence. As a form of self-protection, relationships are approached with a closed heart. They have done this for so long with people it automatically translates into having a closed heart toward God. Spiritual orphans cannot accept what God has for them until the unhealed issues and hidden sources of pain within them are addressed. Constant mistrust was indeed an area of challenge for me. It took some time, the consistent love of God, and prayer before I was truly delivered.

Because of their non-trusting attitude, spiritual orphans become lone rangers. They find it difficult to submit to any form of authority, primarily because submission involves having an open heart, which involves trust, the removal of psychological walls, full integrity of self, inward truth, and honesty in relationships—all virtues blocked by the fear of abandonment, deep unre-solved emotional wounds, and the bruising of the soul by the battle axe of bitterness. Submission is an act of humility, vulnerability, and acceptance that God's grace is sufficient. Submission has the power to set us free from our fears and insecurities, but we have to open our hearts for it to have any value.

Spiritual orphans have an independent spirit—not an interdependent spirit—which often causes them to hide or deny pain or the need for any kind of assistance. If they are not in control, they are in emotional tur-moil. They tend to manipulate relationships, not for the sake of manipulation but in order to feel in control, and if they don't feel in control, they respond with either anger, passivity, isolation, or various other negative coping mechanisms. Orphans are also masters at decep-tion. They are chameleons—able to change to suit their surroundings and environment. They keep their dis-tance from those who are in authority and from those who are able to help them, because they don't want their weaknesses, handicaps, or tenderness to be exposed, exploited, or misused.

Spiritual orphans often find comfort in titles and their identity in material possessions. They are good at "looking" successful because they are focused on out-side appearances. Meanwhile they struggle to deal with the pain inside of them. They also have the tendency to anesthetize themselves through addictions to alcohol, drugs, food, entertainment, work, exercise, and other forms of escape or amusement; they self-validate by seeking recognition, praise, and positions of authority they self-promote by manipulating others to feel they have power over their own lives, even though they are truly out of control in so many ways.

They are big on acts and poor on true intimacy. In their limited understanding love is not received but earned, and no matter what they do they are not good enough to receive it. Their twisted belief system tells them that they have to work for the love of God—that they need to continually do more in order to be accepted by God. They are deceived into believing that they will never measure up to God's standard because they can never do enough or be good enough to attain His love and acceptance, even though He has freely given it to them from the start.

Spiritual orphans can easily become slaves to religion and can't see themselves as sons or daughters of God. Slaves perform duties and tasks while sons and daughters receive the love of the Father, who gives them an understanding of their true identity and introduces them to their rightful inheritance. Sons and daughters serve out of compassion and gratitude. Slaves work hard for the fickle approval of others, and when they receive it, the satisfaction is

> " In Christ we are not the orphans standing out in the snow looking in through the window at the family having Christmas dinner; we are seated at the banquet table. "

only fleeting, forcing them back into a never-ending cycle of trying to earn love and acceptance—like a hamster running on a wheel.

The lifestyle of a spiritual orphan is a case study in legalism, dysfunctional relationships, and missing purpose. They have no sense of direction or destiny. They have shallow and superficial relationships. They live their lives by going through the motions—running in circles, in constant motion but making no progress. They are constantly drawing near to others because of their need for intimate relationship, but then back away for fear of being hurt or rejected.

They are plagued by a constant sense of failure—nothing is ever quite good enough. They are driven to succeed, win, and prove themselves, oftentimes at all costs. They have trouble with personal boundaries, being either too clingy, too forward, or too distant. When bitterness enters, they abandon relationships, jobs, churches, families, and sometimes even communities—running away from those who love them the most to avoid the risk of being betrayed or rejected.

If you see any of these characteristics in yourself, know that the Holy Spirit has the power to set you free. Whether you "feel" accepted or not, if you have accepted Christ, He has accepted you and adopted you into His family. The Scriptures tell us:

> He has granted to us his precious and very great promises, so that through them you may become partakers of the divine nature, having escaped

> from the corruption that is in the world because
> of sinful desire.
>
> —2 PETER 1:4, ESV

Choose to replace your orphan spirit with the spirit of an adopted son or daughter. If you will accept the spirit of adoption and embrace your position as a son or daughter of God, you will be enabled by the Holy Spirit to develop a deeper and deeper relationship with a loving heavenly Father. If you allow Him to put His finger in the hidden places of your heart so that you can be healed and restored, you will also have deeper and more lasting relationships with others. It is His desire for us to experience more than an outer-court relationship. In Christ we are not the orphans standing out in the snow looking in through the window at the family having Christmas dinner; we are seated at the banquet table.

BEING AN INSIDER WITH GOD

God desires intimacy, and that involves an inner-court relationship. An inner-court relationship involves trust and vulnerability. The Father wants us inside with Him. We are no longer outsiders.

As the sons and daughters of God, we have a position that carries privilege and spiritual authority. The body of Christ has not been fully operating in its God-given authority because we are still functioning as spiritual orphans rather than sons and daughters.

Jesus was declared the Son of God by His Father on the day of His baptism:

It came to pass that Jesus also was baptized; and while He prayed, the heaven was opened. And the Holy Spirit descended in bodily form like a dove upon Him, and a voice came from heaven which said, "You are My beloved Son; in You I am well pleased."

—LUKE 3:21–22

Baptism represents death and resurrection. Baptism is a going down, a submitting unto death, and an immersion into. Resurrection can only take place after a death experience. After Jesus was baptized, symbolizing His death and resurrection, the Father made a decree from heaven to the world that Jesus was His beloved Son. Jesus was now ready to represent Him on the earth in all of His power and authority.

The Father in heaven is now waiting to decree His fatherhood to not only the world but also to the principalities and powers of hell. When God the Father decrees that we are His children as a result of the spiritual death and resurrection we underwent when we accepted Christ, the demons in hell will tremble, because we will walk in the true authority and power of God, just as Jesus did. Certainly we have some growing to do before we can be like Jesus, but our aim is always to take on more and more of His character. Jesus was the one who said, "Most assuredly, I say to you, he who believes in Me, the works that I do he will do also; and greater works than these he will do, because I go to My Father" (John 14:12).

To experience the purpose, power, and identity we have in Christ, we must die to the orphan spirit. We must die to doing our own thing or following our own will. We must die to any and all ungodly beliefs that keep us from walking in our position as sons and daughters of God. Our true, royal nature is longing to be resurrected, quickened, and equipped so that we can claim our spiritual inheritance. The Scripture says:

> When He had by Himself purged our sins, sat down at the right hand of the Majesty on high, having become so much better than the angels, as He has by inheritance obtained a more excellent name than they.
>
> —HEBREWS 1:3–4

What is this verse saying? What name did Jesus obtain through His death and resurrection? He obtained the name "Son [or child] of God." In the next chapter we will look at exactly how we can embrace the spirit of adoption.

———

We know what we are, but not what we may be.[2]
—WILLIAM SHAKESPEARE

CHAPTER 6

EMBRACING THE SPIRIT
OF ADOPTION

*Therefore you are no longer a slave but a son [or daughter],
and if a son [or daughter], then an heir of God through Christ.*
—**GALATIANS 4:7**

WE ALL COME into the world with a deficit—a kind of hole in our souls that can only be filled as we relate to others. There is something that we need from the very beginning, and we spend a lifetime trying to compensate for it through our relationships. It is a need that can only be met a little at a time, a day at a time, and we can't go very long without feeling the need to fill this void. It is a need that if not met in the right ways, can drive us into desperation and cause us to make painful decisions. What is this deficit? It is the need for acceptance and to make a genuine connection with others.

When we are infants, we cry for it. As we enter the toddler years, we run toward it as fast as our little legs can carry us. Throughout our childhood and into our teen years we search it out wherever we go making friends, finding mentors, and emulating role models. As we reach adulthood, we look for soul mates to partner with—most intimately in marriage but also in business, society, and in pursuit of building a better world. We attach to political parties and community organizations, add our names to social causes, and even become fans of certain sports teams or celebrities in order to find a place to fit in with like-minded people. We long to belong, and this driving force can lead us to great things—in fact, we can't find true success without it. But it can also lead us to despair, heartache, and defeat if we, as the song says, go looking for love in all the wrong places.

In 2003 the Commission on Children at Risk issued a report they titled *Hardwired to Connect*. Through their research, they put forward the following theory outlining the two basic needs of every human soul. First, a great deal of evidence shows that we are hardwired for close attachments to other people, beginning with our mothers, fathers, and extended families, and then moving out to the broader community. Second, a less definitive but still significant body of evidence suggests that we are hardwired for meaning. We are born with a built-in capacity and drive to search for purpose and reflect on life's ultimate ends.[1]

Another way to look at this is when God created us, He built into us a cavity where He Himself would fit into our lives. Many Christian teachers have called this "a God-sized hole." We were created so we would never be complete without connecting with God, and by extension we would then have dreams and aspirations so great that we could never accomplish them on our own.

For example, having a family, building a business, or changing a community or nation will rarely happen by someone who has hermitted himself away. This need to connect in order to live for a purpose greater than simply meeting our own needs and desires is stitched into the very fabric of our souls.

> " We must allow the Holy Spirit... to rule and reign in our lives so that we can be set free and healed by His supernatural power. "

We are very much like those atoms floating around in the universe that need other atoms so that they can join together and create the building blocks of the cosmos. The molecules of everything we see and that allow life to exist are dependent on these atoms finding one another and joining together. Our relationships seem to have the same significance.

If you have experienced painful relationships that have left you numb, non-trusting, and empty, there is hope. As you begin to cultivate a relationship with God, you will find that He will never leave your or forsake you. He will pour the healing balm of love and fill the empty places and repair the hole in your soul.

Accept the Father's love for you. Don't blame God for the hurt you have experienced. Receive His love and forgiveness through Jesus's blood. We can no longer choose to remain spiritual orphans instead of sons and daughters of God. We must allow the Holy Spirit to fill the hole, to rule and reign in our lives so that we can be set free and healed by His supernatural power. We must give ourselves completely to the Lord, withholding nothing from Him, as the Scriptures prescribe:

> Therefore submit to God. Resist the devil and he will flee from you. Draw near to God and He will draw near to you. Cleanse your hands, you sinners; and purify your hearts, you double-minded. Lament and mourn and weep! Let your laughter be turned to mourning and your joy to gloom. Humble yourselves in the sight of the Lord, and He will lift you up.
>
> —JAMES 4:7–10

Jesus's main purpose was to reveal the Father to us. Jesus always said, "I do nothing of Myself; but as My Father taught Me, I speak these things" (John 8:28). Ask the Holy Spirit to minister to you and reveal the Father to you! Begin by praying the following prayer:

> *Dear Father God, I ask that by Your Holy Spirit You reveal to me Your love and care for me. I lay aside every insecurity, fear, and rejection that has plagued my soul. Heal my wounded heart. Deliver me from repressed emotions hidden in the deepest recesses of my mind. I declare the spirit of an orphan is broken off my life, and I receive the spirit of adoption that cries out, "Abba, Father!" In the name of Jesus, I declare I*

am Your child. I love You, dear Jesus. Thank You
for healing me. Amen.

Now worship your Father in heaven. Listen to some worship songs about God the Father and allow Him to reveal Himself to you! He will transform your life, as the Scripture says: "Nevertheless when one turns to the Lord, the veil is taken away. Now the Lord is the Spirit; and where the Spirit of the Lord is, there is liberty. But we all, with unveiled face, beholding as in a mirror the glory of the Lord, are being transformed into the same image from glory to glory, just as by the Spirit of the Lord" (2 Cor. 3:16–20).

SONS AND DAUGHTERS OF GOD

We live in a fatherless and motherless society. Jesus knew we would suffer with doubt about belonging to the family of God because of the pervasiveness of dysfunction in our natural families. He knew the church would generate thousands of spiritual leaders but not many fathers. He also knew that the church would also produce thousands of mentors but not many mothers, so He promised to give us the spirit of adoption—the very Spirit of God, who teaches us how to pray and gives us the confidence to cry "Abba, Father."

> " Our spirits cease to feel orphaned when we have confidence that we belong to a family—especially God's family. "

Under the laws of America, Australia, and England, an adopted child has certain privileges assigned to them that even natural offspring are not afforded. For example, you cannot disown an adopted child. You cannot disinherit him. He has equal share in the last will and testament of the parent(s) with any natural children. This gives the adopted child unshakable confidence that he will always belong—at least as far as the law is concerned.

Our spirits cease to feel orphaned when we have confidence that we belong to a family—especially God's family. God will never disinherit or disown you. You will have equal share in the common wealth left as your inheritance. Anyone can work hard to earn a salary—they can even become rich—but only a son or daughter can receive an inheritance. And there are things that can only be obtained by inheritance—by being part of a family. This is the blessedness and privilege extended to every child of God—God has secured your inheritance (Eph. 1:3–14).

As true children of God, we must rid ourselves of the orphan mentality and receive confidence from Christ that we are His. Our behavior always betrays what we truly believe. If we behave as if we are still under bondage to the law trying to earn love and acceptance, we are orphans still. If we must work to be pleasing to God, if we must achieve some great and lofty status or work to gain His favor, if we must obey this or that legal requirement to be acceptable, then we still have an orphan spirit.

Conversely, if we behave as a son or daughter, then we will live from that perspective. God the Father owns the land. It is His business, and one day we will inherit it. So we work without guilt or an excessive need to please. We work for Him because it is our pleasure to work out of gratitude and confidence.

So how would I describe the spirit of adoption? I would say it is a mind-set that embraces the following statements:

- I am accepted.
- I belong.
- I am included.
- I am known.
- I am desired.
- I am wanted.
- I am cherished.
- I am treasured.

With the spirit of adoption comes the certainty of:

- God's goodness as your heavenly Father
- Your security as His child
- Your identity in Christ

How do we make this shift? If you don't believe that God is good, fix your eyes on the character of God. Check the adoption papers of His Word—rivet your thoughts and your imagination onto the truth of Scripture.

> The LORD, the LORD God, merciful and gracious, longsuffering, and abounding in goodness and truth, keeping mercy for thousands, forgiving iniquity and transgression and sin.
>
> —EXODUS 34:6–7

> If you then, being evil, know how to give good gifts to your children, how much more will your Father who is in heaven give good things to those who ask Him!
>
> —MATTHEW 7:11

> Do not fear, little flock, for it is your Father's good pleasure to give you the kingdom.
>
> —LUKE 12:32

> If any of you lacks wisdom, let him ask of God, who gives to all liberally and without reproach, and it will be given to him.
>
> —JAMES 1:5

> For men indeed swear by the greater, and an oath for confirmation is for them an end of all dispute. Thus God, determining to show more abundantly to the heirs of promise the immutability of His counsel, confirmed it by an oath, that by two immutable things, in which it is impossible for God to lie, we might have strong consolation, who have fled for refuge to lay hold of the hope set before us.

This hope we have as an anchor of the soul,
both sure and steadfast.
—HEBREWS 6:16–19

MINISTERING TO SOMEONE WITH AN ORPHAN SPIRIT

Perhaps you know someone who is functioning under an orphan spirit. If that is the case, then you must pray, because prayer puts us in touch with the God who answers. If you ask Him, God will direct your prayers. Here is one example of how you might pray:

Father, I pray for (insert name) and ask You to release (insert name) from the negative effect of the orphan spirit. I release the Holy Spirit to hover over him; to love him; to bring healing, deliverance, and a deeper sense of being accepted into Your family. Lord, You are our Father, and I pray that he will receive the spirit of adoption You have promised. I pray that he will feel such love that he will trust You enough to call You, "Abba, Daddy." Grant him the ability to establish a new level of trust and intimacy with You.

Lord, I pray that healing will come to every area of his life. Remove sadness, pain, and hurt. Wash away feelings of abandonment from his heart and heal his emotions. Remove the feelings of isolation, abandonment, and detachment. Help him to trust again. Bring into his life authentic and mutually beneficial relationships. Help him to overcome self-destructive behaviors and addictions. According to Ezekiel 11:19, where his heart has become stony, I pray that You would make it a heart of flesh.

Lord, I ask that You will bring committed spiritual fathers and mothers into his life to cover him in prayer, to give him direction, and to love him unconditionally with the love of Christ. I ask these things in Jesus's name, amen.

It is likely you will be one of the only people praying for this spiritual orphan. It's not unusual for spiritual orphans to have very little spiritual covering because they constantly reject it. Even if you do not see any results, keep praying for him or her. Most of these individuals do love Jesus, but they have been deeply hurt and are functioning out of a woundedness that has made them vulnerable to the enemy.

RECEIVING THE FATHER'S LOVE

If you believe you have been functioning from an orphan spirit, then you have an exciting journey ahead of you. Once you realize this is you, you cannot stay where you are—you must make changes. Healing requires action on your part. You must "walk out" the instructions God gives you. Sometimes this means you will have to just "stick it out" even when things do not feel good or when you are getting negative feedback from others. You must take responsibility for your past actions and attitudes— many of which are the very ones that led you to the place you are right now. You cannot control another person's attitude toward you, but you can control your attitude in any given circumstance.

You must find a church—a healthy Bible church—join that church, and make a commitment to the community and leadership of that house. You must commit yourself to communicating—listening to and sharing—with a loving, accepting spiritual leadership. You must be prepared to receive alignment and direction from your spiritual fathers and mothers on the staff and in the congregation. Love is correction, adjustment, and alignment as much as it is affirmation. A good place to start is by praying the following prayer:

> *Father God, I receive Your love. Although it is difficult to totally trust, help me to overcome psychological and emotional barriers that prohibit me from truly embracing Your unconditional love for me.*
>
> *Please help and empower me to overcome the attitudes, actions, and spirit of an orphan. Your desire for me is that I am a healthy part of a community. I break all unhealthy soul ties I have formed as a result of an orphan spirit, in Jesus's name. I bind my body, heart, mind, and spirit to Your will and purpose for my life. Help me to know the difference between loneliness and aloneness and to recognize that it is not good for me to use food, drugs, or other*

*addictive behaviors and substances to anesthe-
tize my pain, hurt, and disappointments.*

*Heal me from indifference. Help me to remove
the walls, barriers, and psychological defenses
that make it difficult for me to feel loved.*

*Lord, I ask that You would heal my mind and
my heart from the spirits of abandonment, rejection, divorce, abuse, and fatherlessness. Forgive
those who should have been emotionally available
to me but were not. Forgive me for my own indifference toward my family. Help me to love. Please
help me to have the heart of a son (or daughter).
Please help me to turn my heart toward the spiritual fathers and mothers You've placed in my life.
Lord, please reveal to me all of the areas in my life
that have been wounded. Heal those areas and
make me whole. I ask that You would help me to
forgive anyone who has wounded me or failed me.
In Jesus's name I pray, amen.*

What Christ wants you to know today is that you are
not left as an orphan from the love, covenant, and pro-
visions of the Father. In our Lord's own words we have
this promise:

And I will pray the Father, and He will give you
another Helper, that He may abide with you
forever—the Spirit of truth, whom the world
cannot receive, because it neither sees Him nor
knows Him; but you know Him, for He dwells

with you and will be in you. I will not leave you
orphans; I will come to you.

—JOHN 14:16–18

What an assurance! Jesus never leaves us alone. He
sent the Holy Spirit to keep His presence real in our
lives. As Scripture promises: "For He Himself has said,
'I will never leave you nor forsake you.' So we may boldly
say: 'The LORD is my helper; I will not fear. What can
man do to me?'" (Heb. 13:5–6).

God has given to us the spirit of adoption that we
might truly become His children as He promised in
Romans 8:15: "For you did not receive the spirit of
bondage again to fear, but you received the Spirit of
adoption by whom we cry out, 'Abba, Father.'" What an
awesome provision that we might eternally be part of
the family of God as adopted sons and daughters. This
is your true identity—you are a child of the King!

The value of identity, of course, is that
so often with it comes purpose.[2]

—RICHARD GRANT

CHAPTER 7

BREAKING FREE FROM ABUSE

Courage is not the absence of fear, but rather the judgment that something else is more important than fear.[1]
—AMBROSE REDMOON

ABUSE IS DEFINED as the mistreatment of something or someone, and manifests itself in various forms:

- Physical (punching; hitting; slapping; pinching; shaking; less-than-adequate care and support; and improper administration of drugs, treatments, or medication)

- Psychological (repeatedly making someone feel unhappy, anxious, afraid, humiliated, or devalued)

- Sexual (acts that involve physical or non-physical harassment, precludes consent, or the power imbalance is too great for their consent to be considered valid)

- Financial or material (the misuse of a vulnerable person's money, property, possessions, or insurance, or blocking access to these material goods; denying the rights of a competent adult to complain, to vote, or to seek independent legal advice; and stealing a vulnerable person's money, property, possessions, or insurance; or extortion through threats and misappropriation)

- Institutional (the practice of an abusive regime or culture that destroys the dignity and respect to which every person is entitled and occurs when the individual's wishes and needs are sacrificed for the smooth running of an institution, organization, or home)

- Social (intentional or unintentional exclusion from a valued activity, denial of access to community events/groups, or denied access to friends and family)

- Discriminatory (oppressive and discriminatory attitudes toward a person's disability, including physical or learning disability, ill mental health, or sensory impairment; race; age; gender; religion; or cultural background)

The pain of abuse can cause people to give their personal power away. Because of the wrongs perpetrated against them they begin to think they have no control over their lives and instead allow people and circumstances to control their reality. It takes courage to regain it. Courage is the resolve to do something or become something despite fear, hardship, obstacles, and opposition. Courage allows you to accept your fear, embrace it as a legitimate emotion, and use it as fuel to accomplish specific goals.

It takes courage—and a lot of it—to overcome the humiliation, embarrassment, pain, stigma, and shame that comes with abuse. Courage gives you that unction to push through those moments when giving up seems the best option. Courage is the drive that causes you to persevere with firm conviction and rock-solid faith when your confidence is low and the drive to escape is high. It takes courage to endure despite pressing circumstances, unintended consequences, fear, and missteps mixed with the shame and self-doubt that these experiences precipitate.

> " Courage is manifested when you develop a healthy, realistic perspective of who you are in Christ. "

If you are to do something great, it takes courage—courage to stand strong despite failure, opposition, and ridicule. It takes courage to stand up for what is right. It takes courage to stand against all odds and to resist the temptation to compromise morals and convictions in exchange for popularity or influence. It takes courage to move beyond the familiar, that which is guaranteed, and that which gives a sense of security in order to pursue your higher calling. It takes courage to go out on a limb when playing it safe is what others expect.

It takes courage to leave the shores of certainty to become the Christopher Columbus of your life, sailing toward destiny's ever-shifting new horizons. It takes courage to chart a new course when others insist that embracing the status quo is a safer, more sure way to secure success. When I think of this kind of courage, I think of Mahatma Gandhi, Nelson Mandela, Mother Teresa, and Martin Luther King, Jr. I also think of Moses, King David, and Esther. More personally I think of my first mentor, my own mother, as well as my first coach and my sister, Marilyn, who despite lack and the poverty that plagued our lives, defied all odds to complete two college degrees. She would be the first in my family to attend college and set the standard for the rest of us to follow.

Courage comes in all shapes and sizes: Rosa Parks, who refused to sit in the back of the bus, the young man who single-handedly stood down tanks in Tiananmen Square, or the teenage girl who chose not to terminate her pregnancy despite the pressures of the prevailing culture in which she lived.

The courage that overcomes all fear is the courage that is born of God. It is He who places the divine courageous gene within you—the essence of the power to overcome. He has not given you the spirit of fear but of power (2 Tim. 1:7). Look deeply within yourself and you will find it. As the Bible states in 1 John 4:4:

> You belong to God....You have already won a victory...because the Spirit who lives in you is greater than the spirit who lives in the world.
>
> —NLT

Courage is manifested when you develop a healthy, realistic perspective of who you are in Christ—and when you realize all that your Creator has wired you to become and to do. Sadly many people acquiesce to being the slave of unfounded fear instead. Unfounded or baseless fear is a peculiar state of dis-ease in your imagination and arises largely out of a lack of knowledge. As Hosea 4:6 says, "People are destroyed for lack of knowledge."

I believe that not only do we dwindle away and die carrying seeds of greatness, unrealized potential, unpublished best sellers, unsung melodies, undiscovered medical breakthroughs, undeveloped theories and philosophies, undelivered inventions and market solutions, as well as other world-changing insights, but also our lack of knowledge causes divine opportunities and strategic relationships to wither before they ever come to fruition. These opportunities await someone with the courage to do what no one else has done before and who will take on the problems undiscovered innovations and unrealized relationships will solve.

Gaining Strength and Courage

Albert Einstein, in a letter to a professor emeritus of philosophy at the College of the City of New York, defended the appointment of Bertrand Russell to a teaching position with these words:

> Great spirits have always encountered violent opposition from mediocre minds. The mediocre mind is incapable of understanding the man who

refuses to bow blindly to conventional prejudices and chooses instead to express his opinions courageously and honestly.[2]

Courage will cause you to set plausible goals and dare to exceed expectations. Courage is what it takes to accomplish your dreams and visions. Courage is the womb from which great leaders, innovators, activists, and trailblazers are birthed. Courage causes great achievers and champions to look within themselves to find the mental, moral, emotional, and spiritual strength to realize their goals, reach their fullest potential, alter their destinies, and prevail over hardship, pain, disappointment, failure, moral challenges, and mortal danger.

All of us face something that challenges us. All of us face some kind of fear. It could be fear of people, fear of being alone, fear of rejection, fear of failure, fear of change, or fear of commitment. Even people we may perceive as not having any fear at all have had moments when they've had to push past fear.

The blessing does not lie in having no fear, because there are healthy kinds of fear, such as the fear of God. The blessing lies in the effort you make to become mentally, emotionally, and spiritually stronger at what you are wired to do so that you are empowered to face and conquer your unique fears. Eleanor Roosevelt said, "The danger lies in refusing to face the fear, in not daring to come to grips with it.... You must make yourself succeed every time. You must do the thing you think you cannot do."[3] Someone once said to me, "Feel the fear and do it any way." This is real courage.

God gave Joshua the encouragement he needed, and he went on to become one of the most powerful commanders the nation of Israel ever had. He had to learn the art of conditioning his mind to succeed and win by abiding by God's laws of life and living. God advised him, "Be strong and of good courage" (Josh. 1:9).[4]

You must learn the art of mental conditioning. You must develop mental toughness. You must exercise your mind until it aligns with God's Word of truth. Peter's epistle urges you to "gird up the loins of your mind" (1 Pet. 1:13). In other words, don't quit by giving in to your fears. Assume the position of a disciplined warrior and embrace the conqueror you are in Christ! (See 1 Corinthians 15:57.)

> The difference between a successful person and a failure is…that one has the courage to act on his or her ideas, convictions, and beliefs…and the other does not.

How many times did God say, "Be not afraid" throughout the Old and New Testaments? If you hope to change your circumstances, you need courage. If you plan to walk away from an abusive relationship, you'll need courage. If you are going to start a new business, you will need courage. To stand up for yourself and face your giants requires courage.

Whatever God has placed in your spirit to do or to

become, take courage and do it—become it! Go ahead, face your fear and proceed despite opposition. You can and are well able. Be strong and courageous and you will be prosperous and successful. God has promised it, and I not only believe in His promises, I believe in you!

The difference between a successful person and a failure is not that one has better abilities or ideas, superior education or knowledge, the right pedigree, or even an abundance of temporal resources. The difference is that one has the courage to act on his or her ideas, convictions, and beliefs, and to take calculated risks despite the presence of fear, intimidation, or trepidation—and the other does not. Which will you choose to be?

As we are told in the Latin proverb: *"Audentes fortuna juvat; fortes fortuna juvat"*—Fortune favors the bold; fortune favors the brave. And as the Bible urges, "Continue to be bold for Christ" (Phil. 1:20, NLT)—"Be bold . . . and GOD be with you as you do your best" (2 Chron. 19:11, THE MESSAGE).

Remember the words God spoke to Joshua: "Have I not commanded you? Be strong and of good courage; do not be afraid, nor be dismayed, for the LORD your God is with you wherever you go" (Josh. 1:9).

———————

Success is not final, failure is not fatal: it is
the courage to continue that counts.[5]
—AUTHOR UNKNOWN

CHAPTER 8

CHOOSING TO FORGIVE
AFTER BETRAYAL

When you forgive, you in no way change the
past—but you sure do change the future.[1]
—BERNARD MELTZER

BETRAYAL CAN BE debilitating. It robs a person of his or her trust in something or someone through the violation of covenant, contracts, or verbal agreements. If you've ever been betrayed, you know that it can cause intense grief of the soul.

Betrayal of any kind hurts, whether it is on a personal, professional, or even national level. It hurts when a Christian leader breaks trust with his congregation by engaging in immoral behavior. It hurts when politicians lie and cheat for selfish gain. It hurts when a business associate swindles you out of profits. But the worst kind of betrayal is the betrayal of a spouse or close friend. Betrayal by the ones we love—family, friends, business or ministry colleagues, and mentors or confidants—can be so disorienting, it can cause us to forfeit divine opportunities and ministries, and prevent us from maximizing our potential and reaching our destiny.

When someone is betrayed, they often respond in anger or they continually replay what happened, wanting to see the parties who wronged them feel the same or worse emotions they do. This may feel natural, but responding to betrayal in this way will only lead to more bondage, torment, and pain.

My mother used to say that many people are afraid of their own shadows. I would alter that saying just a bit. It seems people spend their lives shadow boxing, trying to fight off memories of the past only to find that it is a waste of time. Like a shadow, repressed memories and suppressed emotions seem to have a will of their own and surface without being summoned.

Like a boiling kettle, we all need a release valve. But how you deal with betrayal is key to living a life of freedom. Trying to get back at the offender is like jumping from a frying pan into fire. The key to overcoming betrayal and dealing with other painful memories is in learning to continuously forgive those who have hurt or offended you. This is perhaps one of the hardest things to do, but forgiveness is vital if you want to be whole. Forgiveness is not about the offender but about you.

In Matthew 18:21–22 Peter came to Jesus with a very provocative question about forgiveness. He said:

> "Lord, how often shall my brother sin against me, and I forgive him? Up to seven times?" Jesus said to him, "I do not say to you, up to seven times, but up to seventy times seven."

Forgiveness is not necessarily a one-time event. You will likely have to repeatedly forgive a person who has wounded you. Let me challenge you with this: every time the memory of the person who hurt you or a painful event comes to your mind, pray, "Lord, I forgive (insert name). Release my soul from the pain associated with this event. Heal my memory in Jesus's name."

The first few times you do this may feel false, but forgiveness is not a feeling. It is an act of your will. As you consistently choose to forgive instead of keeping those negative emotions alive, you will find your anger and hatred begin to subside.

Keep in mind that forgiveness does not mean you totally dismiss or condone wrong and hurtful behavior. It simply means you no longer seek to get even or to punish the person. It means you can pray for God to bless him or her and truly mean it.

If you want to be whole, you must put your best spiritual, psychological, and emotional energies into the healing process and not into keeping the negative emotions of hatred and bitterness alive through unforgiveness. As Lewis Smedes said, "To forgive is to set a prisoner free and discover that the prisoner was you."[2]

I once read the story of the late South African President Nelson Mandela's challenge to forgive. After spending more than twenty years in prison for his anti-apartheid activism, he saw apartheid come to an end, and he eventually became the nation's first black president. At his inauguration Mandela invited the warden of the prison where he'd spent so many years and sat him front and center. As journalist Deroy Murdock observed, "While most people would be tempted to lock up their jailers if they had the chance, Mandela essentially forgave him while the whole world and his own people, white and black, were watching. This quietly sent South Africa's white population a message: Calm down. This will be okay. It also signaled black South Africans: Now is no time for vengeance. Let's show our former oppressors that we are greater than that and bigger people than they were to us."[3]

"Resentment," Mandela once said, "is like drinking poison and then hoping it will kill your enemies."[4]

Instead of dwelling on past pain, begin to see yourself where you want to go. (See Genesis 13:14–18.) Visualize the new life you want—freed from the poison of resentment, the prison of bitterness, and the control of seething anger. See yourself in the future happy, liberated, maximizing your potential, fulfilling your purpose, serving God, and making a difference in this world, free of this pain and suffering.

If you're finding it hard to think positively of the person who hurt you, keep the following quotes in mind:

> The one thing you can't take away from me is the way I choose to respond to what you do to me.[5]
> —VIKTOR E. FRANKL

> The weak can never forgive. Forgiveness is the attribute of the strong.[6]
> —MAHATMA GANDHI

Those who are the hardest to love need it the most.[7]

—SOCRATES

Hurting people hurt people.

—ANONYMOUS

Follow peace with all men, and holiness.

—HEBREWS 12:14, KJV

As far as possible, without surrender, be on good terms with all persons.[8]

—MAX EHRMANN

When memories of those who have hurt, abused, betrayed, or violated you flood your thoughts, and when you cannot seem to forget their evil actions toward you, begin to pray blessings over them. I know this is counterintuitive, but it is biblical. To curse someone means that the curse will have to flow through you first. To bless someone means the blessing will flow through you first. Remember, vengeance belongs to God and there will be a day of judgment. Scripture says:

Dearly beloved, avenge not yourselves, but rather give place unto wrath: for it is written, Vengeance is mine; I will repay, saith the Lord.

Therefore if thine enemy hunger, feed him; if he thirst, give him drink: for in so doing thou shalt heap coals of fire on his head.

Be not overcome of evil, but overcome evil with good.

—ROMANS 12:19–21, KJV

Forgiveness neutralizes the acid of hatred that destroys the person in which it is stored. Get rid of the hate. Forgive your perpetrator and wish him well. The evil we wish upon another tends to have a boomerang effect on us. The same holds true when you are empowered by the Spirit of God to return blessings for hatred. When you are able to bless instead of curse those who have wounded you, you are well on your way to healing the hole in your soul and living a life characterized by wholeness. I know from personal experience that the first few attempts you engage in to release blessings upon people who have hurt you will feel hypocritical. But through repetition you can rewire the natural impulse to seek vengeance yourself.

> Forgiveness neutralizes the acid of hatred that destroys the person in which it is stored.

As we read previously, Jesus instructed His disciples to forgive others seventy times seven. Seventy times seven means to repeat the prayer, "Lord, I forgive (insert name)" over and over again until one day you wake up and notice that it has been weeks, months, or even years since the negative thoughts and angry feelings have surfaced. Forgive again and again until when you see that person, you genuinely wish him well. Eventually the anger and pain that has burned in your heart will evaporate, like dew in the morning sun.

This technique of repetition forces your mind to

overcome the cognitive dissonance between hating someone and acting with compassion toward him. The act of blessing those who hurt you doesn't agree with your feelings of hatred. But since you can't revoke the kind gesture, your mind is forced to change your emotions and thoughts to match your words and actions. Eventually you will begin to say to yourself, "(Insert name) is deserving of a blessing and, indeed, must need one more than I imagined." This is when you know you have truly embraced forgiveness.

You will know that forgiveness has begun
when you recall those who hurt you and
feel the power to wish them well.[9]
—LEWIS B. SMEDES

CHAPTER 9

LEARNING TO BEGIN AGAIN

You must be the change you want to see.[1]
—MAHATMA GANDHI

I ONCE HEARD SOMEONE say that on the day we are born we are given two proverbial envelopes. On the front of one is written incredible pleasure, faith, and prosperity; on the other is written incredible pain, fear, and disease. When opened, each contains the same blank pages called destiny, and we each get to choose the category of pages upon which we will write.

Quoting Andrew Carnegie, author Napoleon Hill expounded on the envelope concept. He said envelope one is labeled "the riches you may enjoy if you take possession of your own mind and direct it to ends of your own choice." Envelope two is labeled "the penalties you must pay if you neglect to take possession of your own mind and direct it."

The first envelope, labeled "riches," includes the blessings:

1. Sound health
2. Peace of mind

3. A labor of love of your own choice

4. Freedom from fear and worry

5. A positive mental attitude

6. Prosperity

The second envelope, labeled "penalties," holds the prices one must pay for neglecting to take possession of one's own mind:

1. Ill health

2. Fear and worry

3. Indecision and doubt

4. Frustration and discouragement throughout life

5. Poverty and want

6. A whole flock of evils consisting of: envy, greed, jealousy, anger, hatred, and superstition[2]

Every day you get to choose the envelope. Which will you choose? Winston Churchill said, "History will be kind to me, for I intend to write it."[3] And write it he did!

Your destiny is connected to your decisions. If you do not like where your life is going, make a decision to change. The earth is a domain that rises and falls on decisions. When God created man, He created him as a free moral agent—a decision-making being. You do not have to see yourself as a victim of circumstance. Indeed, you should not. Where you are today is based on the sum total of decisions you made yesterday. Make a choice to change your situation.

The quality of your life begins and ends with your thoughts. You must take ownership of how and what you think—because therein lies the key to living the life you desire and experiencing the success and prosperity God would have for you.

> " You must take ownership of how and what you think—because therein lies the key to living the life you desire. "

The greatest gifts you can give yourself are the gifts of choice and change. Change is risky business. It may mean that for a while you will have to walk alone. You might have to change your job, change the city in which you live, change the people you hang out with and the places you frequent. Philosopher Herodotus said, "Great deeds are usually wrought at great risks."[4] Change requires decisiveness. Stop hemming and hawing. Think about the option only long enough to determine whether it is worth the effort. If it is, then do it. There is no better time than now.

Choose to have a new beginning now. You cannot go back to your past to have a do-over; life does not work that way. Now is the only time you have, so you might as well start today, at this very moment, to create a new life and a new ending for yourself. Your history does not have to be your destiny. The Scriptures say:

> I call heaven and earth to record this day against
> you, that I have set before you life and death,
> blessing and cursing: therefore choose life, that
> both thou and thy seed may live: That thou mayest
> love the LORD thy God, and that thou mayest
> obey his voice, and that thou mayest cleave unto
> him: for he is thy life, and the length of thy days.
> —DEUTERONOMY 30:19–20

God has given you the power to make decisions that will change your circumstances and reverse the negative conditions in which you live. Wistful and wishful thinking never change anything. As Mahatma Gandhi said, you must be the change you want to see.

Change is not just a process or a principle. It is a person. Jesus Christ is our agent of change. He is the one who gives us the power to change.

In order to see the kind of changes you desire in your life, home, community, ministry, business, government, schools, and nation, you must be intentional. Intentionality is powerful because it refuses to be limited by what is. It forces you to see the possibilities that lie ahead and to find the resources to bring to pass what could be. It forces you to have hope in the future rather than mourning the behaviors, habits, and people we must leave behind. It can be difficult to walk away from maladaptive sets of behaviors and undermining habits. But you must resist the temptation to hold on to them or to take comfort in feeling victimized because that will stagnate your growth and development.

God has prepared an incredible inheritance for you. Choose to accept it! Don't live a shabby life. Don't live in a state of subsistence, just barely getting by. There are greater things in store for you just ahead. Follow the example of the apostle Paul and press toward the mark of the high calling in Christ Jesus (Phil. 3:14)!

> God has given you the power to make decisions that will change your circumstances and reverse the negative conditions in which you live.

I close with an inspiring story that was shared with me. It goes like this: A caretaker faithfully served the lord of a manor for many years. The family of the caretaker had, in fact, served the family of the present lord for many generations. The lord had no heirs, and when he grew older and eventually died, he left the caretaker a suitcase with some documents in it. The caretaker couldn't read, so he put the suitcase away in the attic and forgot about it. Because he had always lived in the little cottage on the estate next to the manor, he continued to live there with his family, and together they kept the house in good repair, the gardens trimmed, and the estate in proper order—working themselves to exhaustion every day, even though no one lived in the big house.

Eventually the caretaker himself was on his deathbed, and his son returned from school to be with him. The caretaker's thoughts turned to the old suitcase, and out of curiosity he told his son where to find it and asked him to read him the papers inside of it. What the son found was the last will and testament of the lord, in which he had left the entire estate to the caretaker! All those years he had lived in the little cottage on the edge of the estate working his fingers to the bone, when he could have moved into the big house and hired others to do the work for him!

In the same way, many of us live in a small corner of our potential, imprisoned by the events of our past, either because we don't realize all we are purposed to be or because we don't realize all we have available to fulfill that purpose. The whole estate of potential is ours, but we look at the obstacles, blockades, and booby traps between the small corner where we are now and the rest of the expanse—and we have no idea how to get from here to there. All we see are the walls and fences between us and our dreams. We believe the lies that these barriers are impenetrable. We accept the "no trespassing" signs put up between the little we now have and the abundance that is rightfully ours. But we can change. The choice is ours.

THE CHOICE IS YOURS

You don't have to remain in a self-imposed prison of failure, pain, shame, or rejection because you struggle in one area or another. You can overcome your past and embrace the freedom and liberty found in Christ Jesus.

Overcoming your past starts with the decision to

take responsibility for your life and to act on the knowledge you have. Take action now. Will Rogers said, "Even if you are on the right track, you will get run over if you just sit there."[5] Don't look back and wish that things were different; you only waste precious time regretting and lamenting, because regret never changes anything.

Author Morty Lefkoe, in his book *Re-Create Your Life*, teaches a simple process that can be used to reinterpret past events:

1. Identify the undesirable pattern.

2. Name the underlying belief and driving factor(s).

3. Identify the source of the belief in memory, including as much sensory (physiological, sensual, relational, social, cultural, and environmental) detail as possible.

4. Describe possible alternate interpretation of the memory. Realize that your original mental model is an interpretation to reality.

5. Address the judgment you have assigned the memory or belief.

6. Consciously choose to reject the original belief as "false."

7. Consciously choose to accept your reinterpretation as "true."[6]

I would add:

1. Forgive.
2. Give yourself the gift of a new beginning.

Remember, you don't have to live your life blinded by the pain of yesterday. There is a direct relationship between your life as a whole and the actions you take every moment of every day. Those moment-by-moment decisions hold the key to

> " Moving forward is not the same as moving on. "

living a happy and liberated life in Christ Jesus. You can be liberated from the law of sin and death if each day you take small, manageable steps toward living the life you desire. Trust the leading of the Spirit of God. He will equip you with the wisdom to make the right decisions based on purpose and God's ultimate plan for your life. In taking these steps you will begin to move beyond your comfort zone.

Moving forward is not the same as moving on. Some people are the same way they were yesterday because they have moved forward but their minds remain paralyzed in the past. Move on toward your goal. Don't lose heart. Keep hope alive and reach out for help when you need it. Develop a solid strategy for change that includes a supportive community of believers, accountability partners, and mutually beneficial relationships.

If there's one certainty in life it's that things will not always go according to plan! But plan anyway. Plan for a brighter future. Trust God in the process. Remember, He will never leave you or forsake you. He has sent His precious Holy Spirit to help you. He will help you to get back on course when you are derailed. As long as you recommit yourself to your goal, you will be able to recover from your mistakes. Go easy on yourself but keep going.

The power to choose is yours: victim or victor, life or death, blessings of cursing, success or failure. (See Matthew 11:12; John 10:10; Deuteronomy 30:19.) In one of my favorite books, *Man's Search for Meaning*, holocaust survivor Viktor E. Frankl said, "Everything can be taken from a man but one thing: the last of the human freedoms—to choose one's attitude in any given set of circumstances, to choose one's own way."[7] God has given you the options. Now the choice is yours.

Do not remember the former things, nor consider the things of old. Behold, I will do a new thing, now it shall spring forth.
—ISAIAH 43:18–19

NOTES

INTRODUCTION

1. Michael Miles, "Taking Responsibility—There Is Always a Choice," Dumb Little Man: Tips for Life, September 13, 2008, http://www.dumblittleman.com/2008/09/taking-responsibility -there-is-always.html (accessed February 19, 2014).

CHAPTER 1—ARE YOU READY FOR THE CHALLENGE?

1. Joni Eareckson Tada, "Joni Eareckson Tada Story," http:// joniearecksontadastory.com/jonis-story-page-1/ (accessed February 20, 2014).

2. Ibid.

3. Ibid.

4. Charlotte Brontë, *Jane Eyre*, The Project Gutenberg, http://www.gutenberg.org/files/1260/1260-h/1260-h.htm (accessed February 20, 2014).

CHAPTER 2—REWIRING YOUR MIND

1. This quote is widely attributed to Albert Einstein, but its origin is in question. In her book *The New Quotable Einstein* (Princeton, NJ: Princeton University Press, 2005), editor Alice Calaprice suggests it may be a variation of this Einstein quote, "A new type of thinking is essential if mankind is to survive and move toward higher levels."

2. B. L. McGinnity, J. Seymour-Ford, and K. J. Andries, "Helen Keller," Perkins History Museum, Perkins School for the Blind (Watertown, MA: 2004), http://www.perkins.org/vision -loss/helen-keller/ (accessed February 20, 2014).

3. Brainyquote.com, "Helen Keller Quotes," http://www .brainyquote.com/quotes/keywords/vision.html (accessed February 20, 2014).

4. Brainyquote.com, "Vision Quotes," http://www .brainyquote.com/quotes/keywords/vision.html (accessed February 20, 2014).

5. Oliver Wendell Holmes, *The Autocrat of the Breakfast-Table*, The Project Gutenberg, http://www.gutenberg.org/files/751/751-h/751-h.htm (accessed February 20, 2014).

6. William T. Powers, as quoted by Josh Kaufman in *The Personal MBA* (New York: Portfolio, 2010).

7. Brainyquote.com, "Anais Nin Quotes," http://www.brainyquote.com/quotes/authors/a/anais_nin.html (accessed February 20, 2014).

8. Horace as quoted in Robert Christy, comp., *Proverbs, Maxims and Phrases of All Ages* (New York: Bartleby, 2010).

9. David C. McCasland, "Defining Moment," April 16, 2008, Our Daily Bread, http://odb.org/2008/04/16/defining-moment/ (accessed February 20, 2014).

CHAPTER 3—BREAKING THE TIES THAT BIND

1. BrainyQuote.com, "Denis Waitley Quotes," http://www.brainyquote.com/quotes/authors/d/denis_waitley.html (accessed February 20, 2014).

2. Roy B. Zuck, *The Speaker's Quote Book* (Grand Rapids, MI: Kregel, 2009), 246.

3. Goodreads.com, "Richard Buckminster Fuller Quotes," https://www.goodreads.com/author/quotes/165737.Richard_Buckminster_Fuller (accessed February 21, 2014).

CHAPTER 4—HEALING THE PAIN OF GUILT AND SHAME

1. John Irving, *A Prayer for Owen Meany* (New York: William Morrow, 1989), 37.

CHAPTER 5—OVERCOMING THE SPIRIT OF AN ORPHAN: REJECTION AND ABANDONMENT

1. UNICEF, "Statistics by Area/HIV-AIDS: Orphans," April 2013, http://www.childinfo.org/hiv_aids_orphanestimates.php?q=printme (accessed February 21, 2014).

2. Goodreads.com, "William Shakespeare Quotes," http://www.goodreads.com/quotes/12236-we-know-what-we-are-but-not-what-we-may (accessed February 21, 2014).

Chapter 6—Embracing the Spirit of Adoption

1. The Commission on Children at Risk, *Hardwired to Connect: The New Scientific Case for Authoritative Communities* (New York: The Institute for American Values, 2003).

2. Brainyquote.com, "Richard Grant," http://www.brainyquote.com/quotes/quotes/r/richardgra185719.html (accessed February 21, 2014).

Chapter 7—Breaking Free From Abuse

1. Goodreads.com, "Ambrose Redmoon Quotes," http://www.goodreads.com/quotes/320373-courage-is-not-the-absence-of-fear-but-rather-the (accessed February 24, 2014).

2. Albert Einstein, letter to Morris Raphael Cohen, professor emeritus of philosophy at the College of the City of New York, March 19, 1940. Einstein is defending the appointment of Bertrand Russell to a teaching position.

3. Eleanor Roosevelt, *You Learn by Living* (New York: Harper Perennial, 2011), 29–30.

4. Adapted from Cindy Trimm, *When Kingdoms Clash* (Lake Mary, FL: Charisma House, 2012), 45–47.

5. This quote is widely attributed to Winston Churchill, but the author is unknown. "Winston Churchill for Traders & Analysts," The Churchill Centre, http://tinyurl.com/mfj7otw (accessed February 24, 2014).

Chapter 8—Choosing to Forgive After Betrayal

1. Brainyquote.com, "Bernard Meltzer Quotes," http://www.brainyquote.com/quotes/authors/b/bernard_meltzer.html#Q7MwvMdorBYrXyZ0.99 (accessed February 12, 2014).

2. Brainyquote.com, "Lewis B. Smedes Quotes," http://www.brainyquote.com/quotes/authors/l/lewis_b_smedes.html (accessed February 24, 2014).

3. Deroy Murdock, "Nelson Mandela, R.I.P.," National Review Online, December 5, 2013, http://www.nationalreview.com/corner/365631/nelson-mandela-rip-deroy-murdock (accessed February 24, 2014).

4. *USA Today*, "15 of Nelson Mandela's Best Quotes," December 6, 2013, http://www.usatoday.com/story/news/nation-now/2013/12/05/nelson-mandela-quotes/3775255/ (accessed February 24, 2014).

5. Goodreads.com, "Viktor E. Frankl Quotes," http://www.goodreads.com/author/quotes/2782 (accessed February 24, 2014).

6. Brainyquote.com, "Mahatma Gandhi Quotes," http://www.brainyquote.com/quotes/authors/m/mahatma_gandhi.html (accessed February 24, 2014).

7. Goodreads.com, "Socrates Quotes," http://www.goodreads.com/quotes/873683-those-who-are-hardest-to-love-need-it-the-most (accessed February 24, 2014).

8. Goodreads.com, "Max Ehrmann Quotes," http://www.goodreads.com/author/quotes/177071.Max_Ehrmann (accessed February 24, 2014).

9. Brainyquote.com, "Lewis B. Smedes Quotes."

CHAPTER 9—LEARNING TO BEGIN AGAIN

1. Brainyquote.com, "Mahatma Gandhi Quotes."

2. Napoleon Hill, "Whatever the Mind Can Conceive, Believe Can Achieve," http://www.youtube.com/watch?v=A3i9pP2wMzc (accessed February 24, 2014).

3. Brainyquote.com, "Winston Churchill Quotes," http://www.brainyquote.com/quotes/authors/w/winston_churchill_2.html (accessed February 24, 2014).

4. Brainyquote.com, "Herodotus Quotes," http://www.brainyquote.com/quotes/authors/h/herodotus_2.html (accessed February 24, 2014).

5. Brainyquote.com, "Will Rogers Quotes," http://www.brainyquote.com/quotes/authors/w/will_rogers.html (accessed February 24, 2014).

6. As referenced in Josh Kaufman, *The Personal MBA* (New York: Penguin Group, 2010).

7. Viktor E. Frankl, *Man's Search for Meaning* (Boston: Beacon Press, 1992), 75.